THE STRAIT OF HORMUZ GAMBIT

THE STRAIT OF HORMUZ GAMBIT

HICHEM KAROUI

CONTENTS

CHAPTER 1

Introduction

The Strait of Hormuz and Global Energy Security

Historical and Geopolitical Context of the Strait of Hormuz

The Strait of Hormuz has always been a key hub for maritime trade, connecting the Arab-Persian Gulf to the Indian Ocean. Over the centuries, this strategic passage has played a crucial role in trade between the East and the West. Ancient civilisations, including the Mesopotamians and Persians, recognised the vital importance of this waterway. However, it is in recent decades that international attention has focused sharply on the security and stability of this key region. With a large share of the world's oil flowing through this narrow strait, the geopolitics of the region have made it a hot topic of concern for regional and international actors. Historical tensions between some of the regional powers, such as Iran, Saudi Arabia and the United Arab Emirates, as well as the global interests of major powers, make the Strait of Hormuz a complex and often volatile geopolitical theatre. Furthermore, recent political and security developments in the region have heightened questions and concerns about the free movement of merchant ships through these strategic waters. In this context, an in-depth analysis of the historical and geopolitical context of the Strait of Hormuz is essential to understand the present and anticipate the future of this region, which is so crucial to the global economy.

The Strategic Challenge: A Crucial Maritime Passage

The Strait of Hormuz, a true geostrategic crossroads, is a crucial maritime passage at the heart of global challenges. Connecting the Arab-Persian Gulf to the Sea of Oman, it spans a maximum width of only 39 kilometres. This narrowness makes the passage vitally important for the transit of energy resources, particularly oil and gas, whose regular flow has major global repercussions.

The geographical location of the Strait of Hormuz poses unparalleled challenges for navigation and maritime security. Trade flows through this sea lane are subject to constant surveillance by multiple regional and international actors. However, political tensions and geopolitical rivalries exacerbate security concerns, weighing on the stability of the region and global markets.

This strategic route is also the scene of power games between major powers seeking to secure access to energy resources while ensuring the free movement of ships in the area. The fragile balance in this sensitive area highlights the major strategic importance of the Strait of Hormuz, forcing international actors to reconsider their positions and alliances.

The protection of economic and geopolitical interests in this crucial region is therefore a key concern for the world's major players. As a result, diplomatic and military developments in the Strait of Hormuz directly influence global energy security, prompting serious reflection on the economic models and security strategies of the states concerned.

Key Players: Regional Powers and International Influence

The turbulent waters of the Strait of Hormuz are steeped in the complexity of relations between regional players and international powers. The proximity of this strategic passage to major countries such as Iran, Oman, the United Arab Emirates and Saudi Arabia makes it a key geopolitical theatre. Each of these actors has specific interests related to energy security, maritime trade and regional influence. Iran, as the predominant regional power, considers partial control of the strait to be a trump card in its political game. At the same time, the Gulf monarchies fear Tehran's rise in power and seek to guarantee the security of their oil exports. This regional rivalry is part of a broader context of clashes of influence between Iran, the United States, China and the European Union. The US military presence in the region, the EU's diplomatic efforts to preserve the nuclear agreement and China's economic ambitions add layers of complexity to this theatre of conflicting interests. The key question is whether the key players will be able to maintain a fragile balance while avoiding the conflagration of a region already marked by conflict. Regional and international collaboration on the management of this vital passage is imperative to prevent any escalation of tensions that would threaten global energy stability. As the situation evolves, interactions between these key players will continue to shape the geopolitics of the Strait of Hormuz and have repercussions on the global balance of power.

Diplomatic Dynamics: Dialogue and Persistent Tensions

The diplomatic dynamics surrounding the Strait of Hormuz, a strategic crossroads of national and international interests, are characterised by nuanced dialogue and persistent tensions. Regional powers such as Iran, the United Arab Emirates and Oman, as well as dominant international actors such as the United States, Russia and China, are engaged in a complex game of negotiations and assertions of influence, while navigating cautiously between cooperation and rivalry. Multilateral dialogues aimed at preserving freedom of navigation and easing economic and political rivalries remain tenuous in the face of historical antagonisms and conflicting aspirations. Diplomatic rhetoric alternates between calls for de-escalation and demonstrations of strength, reflecting a constant search for balance between national interests and regional security imperatives. At the same time, persistent tensions stem from complex geopolitical disputes involving shifting alliances and geostrategic issues that are crucial to global stability. Persistent differences over nuclear agreements, territorial disputes and economic rivalries fuel a climate of mutual mistrust and uncertainty about the future of the vital Strait of Hormuz. In this regard, the diplomatic balance remains fragile, subject to shifting regional and global power dynamics. The intensity of the issues crystallising around the Strait of Hormuz requires continued vigilance and concerted diplomacy to prevent any escalation that could undermine global stability and the global energy balance.

Economic Impact of Oil and Gas Flow

The smooth flow of oil and gas through the Strait of Hormuz has a significant influence on global energy markets and the financial stability of regional players. Fluctuations in this flow have major economic repercussions worldwide, affecting the financial stability of exporting countries, energy costs for end consumers, and the competitiveness of industries dependent on oil and gas.

Volatility in flow, resulting from geopolitical tensions or technical disruptions, creates uncertainty in international markets, leading to rapid price fluctuations and supply insecurity. Even a temporary sharp drop in oil flow can be enough to cause global oil prices to spike, negatively impacting economies that are heavily dependent on this resource. Similarly, a persistent threat to strategic shipping routes hinders the predictability of liquefied natural gas supplies, exacerbating the risk of shortages and price increases.

Beyond immediate fluctuations, uncertainties surrounding oil and gas flows undermine long-term energy investment planning for both producers and consumers. Hesitation in decision-making and constant adjustments to production dynamics are slowing the development of new energy infrastructure, thereby increasing the obstacles to a gradual transition to alternative and renewable sources. This directly impacts the diversification of national economies and greenhouse gas emission reduction targets.

In short, the economic impact of oil and gas flows through the Strait of Hormuz extends far beyond regional borders to shape the contours of the global economy. The security and stability of this strategic passage is therefore crucial to ensuring the smooth flow of energy resources and avoiding turbulence that disrupts global financial stability.

Offshore Infrastructure: Logistical Risks and Resilience

Offshore infrastructure, technological marvels that serve the global energy supply, are at the heart of a complex dance between logistical risks and resilience. These facilities, whether offshore oil or gas platforms, are an essential link in the global energy supply chain, but their safety and uninterrupted operation face a myriad of challenges. Harsh maritime conditions, geopolitical threats, environmental risks and the technical challenges inherent in their operation and maintenance require constant vigilance and cutting-edge expertise. The combination of these factors makes offshore infrastructure particularly sensitive areas, where fragile balances are at play on a daily basis.

The risks to these complex structures are manifold. Violent storms and extreme weather conditions constantly test the structural and operational integrity of these installations. In addition, the presence of coveted energy resources makes them potential targets for sabotage or deliberate attacks, fuelling underlying geopolitical tensions. Furthermore, the protection of the marine environment is crucial, as even the smallest leak or accident can have catastrophic consequences for marine and coastal ecosystems. Finally, the upkeep and maintenance of these infrastructures require highly specialised expertise, which is also a major challenge in a context of limited human resources and staff turnover.

In the face of these risks, the logistical resilience of offshore installations is proving to be a determining factor. Advanced risk monitoring and management systems are being deployed to detect potential threats and anticipate critical situations. In addition, strict safety procedures and incident response protocols are constantly monitored, helping to minimise the consequences of any uncontrolled events. Technological innovation also plays a key role in improving safety standards, with the development of advanced detection devices, resistant materials and cutting-edge engineering practices.

In short, offshore infrastructure is both a vital link in the global energy chain and a fragile territory exposed to a multitude of risks. Securing it and ensuring its uninterrupted operation requires a holistic approach combining technical expertise, international cooperation and ongoing innovation. In a context of energy transition and geopolitical volatility, the sustainability of this infrastructure remains a major challenge for the stability of global energy supplies.

Maritime Security: Cooperation or Confrontation?

Maritime security in the Strait of Hormuz region is a matter of paramount importance, not only for regional actors but also for the rest of the world. The question of whether it should be addressed through cooperation between the various maritime powers or whether it risks turning into direct confrontation is at the heart of the debates and strategies implemented by the actors involved. The porosity of maritime borders, combined with the concentration of oil and gas traffic, creates an environment conducive to tensions and rivalries. In this context, it is imperative to assess the options available to ensure the safety of navigation without compromising regional stability. Cooperation between the naval forces of coastal countries and those of extra-regional powers has been suggested as a possible solution. However, the divergent interests of the actors involved make it difficult to establish such a maritime security mechanism. At the same time, the temptation to resort to unilateral means to protect national interests raises concerns about escalating tensions and the risk of confrontation. Recent incidents, such as ship seizures and aggressive manoeuvres, have fuelled fears of excessive militarisation in the region. Thus, the question of whether maritime security in the Strait of Hormuz will be managed through multilateral cooperation or whether it will lead to potentially dangerous confrontations remains an enigma. A balanced approach, based on dialogue and diplomacy, seems to be the most prudent course of action to avoid a precarious situation of conflict.

Technological Developments: Surveillance and Defence

Technological developments in the field of surveillance and defence have profoundly reshaped the maritime strategies of the actors involved in the security of the Strait of Hormuz. Indeed, rapid advances in artificial intelligence, underwater robotics, sensor networks and surveillance satellites have offered new perspectives for the protection of strategic sea lanes.

The advent of automated surveillance systems has enabled increased vigilance and faster response times to emerging threats. Autonomous vessels equipped with advanced detection technologies have become major assets in securing commercial traffic, providing a discreet but effective presence in the maritime domain.

At the same time, innovations in the field of defence have given rise to new paradigms in deterrence and risk management. Electronic jamming techniques, sophisticated anti-ship missile systems and counter-mine devices have strengthened the ability to protect shipping lanes, while imposing a new balance in the balance of power.

Furthermore, the integration of cybersecurity technologies into defence systems has radically transformed the parameters of maritime conflict. The growing vulnerability of the IT networks of port facilities, oil platforms and command centres has created an imperative for preparedness and resilience in the face of cyber attacks.

However, these technological advances also raise questions about their potential use in confrontational contexts. The proliferation of armed naval drones, stealth submarines and sophisticated electronic warfare capabilities poses major ethical and security challenges, calling for rigorous international regulation to prevent any escalation of tensions.

In the face of these constant developments, multilateral cooperation in the field of surveillance and defence appears to be essential to guarantee the safety of critical maritime routes. Information sharing, the establishment of incident prevention mechanisms and the harmonisation of safety standards are essential levers for collective risk management. In this context, the interoperability of surveillance systems and the coordination of maritime security operations are major priorities in addressing the contemporary challenges of global navigation.

Disruption Scenarios: Analysis and Outlook

When addressing the issue of the Strait of Hormuz and its potential disruption, it is imperative to examine possible scenarios through an analytical lens informed by geopolitical foresight. The first scenario is based on a series of minor incidents temporarily affecting the flow of energy resources through the strait—a challenge that the international community should be able to manage without causing major disruption. However, if these incidents continue or multiply, we could see a second scenario emerge, characterised by prolonged partial disruption, leading to significant economic repercussions and prompting global actors to consider emergency measures to mitigate sudden shortages. Finally, the most extreme scenario, although speculative, envisages a complete strategic transformation of the global energy landscape, with the strait being bypassed by new energy corridors, causing major geopolitical upheaval. These scenarios, although speculative, require serious attention from policymakers and analysts, as they highlight the need to prepare energy mitigation and diversification strategies in the face of potential instability. Thus, the relevant authorities must grasp the crucial importance of understanding these potential disruption scenarios in order to develop effective policies that will help strengthen global energy security in a context of increased volatility.

Global Consequences: The Energy Transition Put to the Test

The prospect of major disruptions in the Strait of Hormuz, and by extension to global energy security, is raising legitimate concerns about the potential consequences for the ongoing energy transition. This period of uncertainty is exacerbating debates and decisions related to investments in renewable energy and reducing dependence on fossil fuels. Crisis scenarios in the Strait of Hormuz highlight the urgent need to diversify energy sources and strengthen infrastructure resilience in the face of such events. Indeed, a prolonged disruption of oil and gas flows through the strait could lead to major economic upheavals, affecting not only the countries directly involved, but also global markets and geopolitical stability. The question of the global consequences of these disruptions raises fundamental issues for the future of the energy transition. On the one hand, a prolonged interruption or significant increase in the costs of hydrocarbon transit could accelerate investment in energy alternatives, such as renewable energies, thereby stimulating innovation and competitiveness in this sector. On the other hand, the repercussions on global markets could lead to additional geopolitical tensions, exacerbating rivalries between regional and international players for access to resources and control of new energy corridors. The energy transition is therefore being tested by these potential scenarios, faced with the need to accelerate its pace while ensuring a fair and peaceful transition. Furthermore, this situation highlights the crucial importance of rethinking global energy governance in order to ensure international cooperation and prevent conflicts over access to strategic resources. In the face of these challenges, it is imperative to adopt an integrated approach, combining economic, political and technological strategies, to shape a resilient and sustainable energy future.

References

Baldwin-Edwards, Martin. *Energy Security in the Gulf: The Future of Oil and Gas Exports from the Arabian Peninsula* . London: Palgrave Macmillan, 2021.

Ehteshami, Anoushiravan, and Naser al-Tamimi. "The Strait of Hormuz and the Gulf's Strategic Significance." *Middle East Policy* 25, no. 3 (2018): 45–62.

U.S. Department of Defense. *Annual Report on Military Power of Iran* . Washington, D.C.: Office of the Secretary of Defense, 2023.

U.S. Energy Information Administration (EIA). "The Strait of Hormuz Is the World's Most Important Oil Transit Chokepoint." Last modified July 26, 2023. https://www.eia.gov/todayinenergy/detail.php?id=57241 .

Growing Tensions

Iran, Israel and the Fragile Balance in the Middle East

Historical Context: Origins of Conflicts and Antagonisms

The Middle East region is marked by a complex colonial legacy, resulting from Western domination and influence over the past centuries. The consequences of the First World War and the break-up of the Ottoman Empire led to the arbitrary redrawing of borders, creating tensions among various ethnic, religious and political groups. Historical rivalries between groups such as Arabs and Persians, as well as sectarian divisions, were exacerbated by this foreign interference, laying the foundations for the current conflicts. The emergence of the State of Israel in 1948 also triggered decades of tension and violence, fuelled by conflicting territorial claims and deep cultural differences. The Israeli occupation of disputed territories has fuelled persistent Palestinian resistance, contributing to regional instability. The interference and geopolitical interests of major world powers, such as the United States and Russia, have added further complexity to this already tumultuous landscape.

Key Players: Regional Powers and Multipolar Influences

The Middle East region is the scene of complex political rivalries involving a multitude of key players, each seeking to promote its strategic interests in an often tumultuous geopolitical landscape. Among these players, Iran stands out as a major regional power, exerting significant influence over affairs in the Middle East. Its involvement in regional conflicts such as the civil war in Syria and disputes in Lebanon, as well as its proximity to Israel, fuel widespread geopolitical tensions. In addition, Iran maintains strategic relations with non-state actors such as Hezbollah, further strengthening its multifaceted influence. At the same time, Israel remains a key force in the region, with proven military capabilities and strong international alliances. Long-standing rivalries between Iran and Israel have created a climate of mistrust and competition that constantly shapes the political landscape of the Middle East. These regional powers operate in a multipolar context in which other international actors are also involved. The United States plays a leading role, providing unwavering support to Israel while adopting a position of mistrust towards Iran. Russia has expanded its spheres of influence by forging strategic partnerships with Iran and other regional players, while China seeks to consolidate its economic interests in the region by developing trade and energy ties. In short, the geopolitical dynamics in the Middle East are strongly influenced by the complex interactions between these regional powers and the multiple international forces operating there, shaping a delicate and unstable balance whose repercussions extend far beyond the region's borders.

Shadow War: Espionage and Cybersecurity

In the corridors of power, modern wars are no longer confined to physical territories, but now extend to digital territories. Espionage and cybersecurity have become major issues in the dynamics of geopolitical tensions in the Middle East. The growing sophistication of cyber capabilities has redefined the boundaries of conflict, introducing a new battlefield where states and non-state actors compete to consolidate their supremacy. In this shadow war, major powers are investing heavily in the development of cyber armies capable of operating in the relative anonymity of cyberspace.

Espionage, meanwhile, is of unquestionable strategic importance. Intelligence agencies are engaged in a relentless struggle to gain access to sensitive information and destabilise their opponents' structures. Clandestine alliances are being forged, disinformation operations are multiplying and networks of infiltrated agents are proliferating. This shadow war is also being waged on the technological front, with the deployment of sophisticated malware designed to undermine defence systems and disrupt critical infrastructure.

At the heart of these issues lies the crucial question of cyber security. Targeted cyber attacks, hacking attempts and digital propaganda campaigns are all threats that states must face in order to preserve their integrity and sovereignty. The quest to develop effective defensive strategies requires cutting-edge expertise and considerable resources, but remains subject to constant change as technology advances.

Thus, the shadow war, whether waged through traditional espionage or cyber operations, further complicates the already fragile balance in the Middle East. It highlights the urgent need for regional and international actors to rethink their strategic approaches and develop regulatory mechanisms adapted to this new conflictual reality.

Religious Tensions and National Identities

Religious tensions and identity conflicts in the Middle East are deeply rooted in the complex history of the region. For centuries, religious differences have often been used as political levers to influence social, political and geopolitical dynamics. Indeed, rivalries between different branches of Islam, Sunni and Shia, as well as historical tensions between Jewish and Muslim communities, contribute to the region's instability. National identities intertwine with these religious tensions, creating a complex environment where territorial claims and nationalist aspirations fuel potential conflicts. Therefore, it is crucial to understand these deep-rooted tensions in order to fully grasp the dynamics of international relations in the Middle East. Religious conflicts and identity claims are often exploited by various state and non-state actors in pursuit of their political and geostrategic interests. The manipulation of national and religious identities creates divisions within societies and exacerbates antagonisms, further weakening the already precarious regional balance. These tensions can also extend beyond national borders, fuelling transnational conflicts and blurring the traditional boundaries of geopolitical issues. Faced with these highly complex challenges, it is imperative to adopt a nuanced approach that recognises both religious and identity realities while seeking avenues for dialogue and reconciliation. Understanding the deep roots of these tensions must guide strategies aimed at resolving crises and establishing lasting foundations for peace and stability in the region. This requires challenging simplistic mindsets and a genuine commitment to recognising cultural and religious diversity. By demystifying stereotypes and promoting an inclusive vision, it is possible to lay the foundations for peaceful and harmonious coexistence based on mutual respect and human dignity.

Diplomacy and Sanctions: A Subtle Balancing Act

Diplomacy and sanctions are a complex arena where delicate balances are at play. In the context of growing tensions between Iran, Israel and other regional actors, diplomatic efforts to contain antagonisms and promote peaceful solutions are essential. However, the imposition of economic sanctions is also a major strategic tool in this delicate balancing act. Sanctions, whether unilateral or multilateral, aim to exert economic and political pressure on a state or group of actors to influence their behaviour. They can take various forms, such as trade restrictions, financial restrictions or export bans. Their impact is significant, affecting both the targeted governments and civilian populations. Thus, the implementation of sanctions requires careful analysis to assess their intended and collateral effects. In the context of the Middle East, where historical rivalries and geostrategic issues are intertwined, the implications of sanctions are profound. Diplomatic negotiations aimed at resolving tensions and avoiding open conflict must contend with the challenges posed by the use of sanctions. International cooperation, particularly within bodies such as the UN and other regional organisations, is central to these dynamics. Reaching consensus on the nature and scope of sanctions is therefore a complex process involving compromise and careful deliberation. Furthermore, efforts to maintain open channels of communication, despite differences, are fundamental to preserving opportunities for dialogue and mediation. The effectiveness of sanctions as an instrument of coercion depends on their credibility and legitimacy. Consequently, diplomatic actions surrounding the imposition and lifting of sanctions are subject to constant re-evaluation. Ultimately, diplomacy and sanctions represent a game in which caution and insight are required. Their complex interaction reveals the nuances of international dialogue and highlights the crucial issues underlying relations between state and non-state actors.

Military Rhetoric: Discourse and Statements

Military rhetoric plays a central role in international relations, particularly when it comes to growing tensions between Iran, Israel and the fragile balance in the Middle East. Speeches and statements by the leaders of these nations have a profound strategic dimension, often intended to strengthen internal legitimacy, deter potential adversaries, or mobilise national and international public opinion.

The language used in military speeches is often laden with symbols and historical references, aimed at placing present actions within a narrative continuum, projecting an aura of power, or even provoking an emotional response in the audience. Political and military leaders thus skilfully wield words, exploiting the power of rhetoric to influence perceptions and attitudes.

In the specific context of the Middle East, where historical and geopolitical rivalries are heightened, military rhetoric takes on a particular significance. Veiled threats, warnings and assertions of strength can lead to an escalation of tensions, stimulate military preparations and influence political decisions. Statements about military capabilities, strategic alliances and operational intentions are never just words thrown into the air, but cornerstones on which the conflictual and cooperative dynamics of the region are built.

However, this rhetoric is not simply an exercise in strategic communication. It is part of a broader context of complex international relations, subject to multifaceted pressures and rapid change. Thus, speeches and statements are not only instruments of intimidation or persuasion, but also signals that international actors deploy to probe their adversaries, assess the limits of escalating tensions, or even explore spaces for dialogue.

It is therefore crucial to analyse military rhetoric with close attention, to understand its practical and symbolic implications, while remaining aware of the subtleties and ambiguities that characterise this fundamental aspect of international relations. The way in which speeches and statements are perceived, interpreted and relayed by different actors – both at the national and international level – can play a decisive role in the trajectory of events and crises that shape the geopolitical theatre of the Middle East.

External influences: the roles of the United States, Russia and China

The geopolitical actions of the United States, Russia and China have a significant influence on the fragile balance in the Middle East. The United States, as a major player on the international stage, has long played a central role in the region, often supporting Israel and opposing Iranian influence. Its military presence and strategic alliances have helped shape the complex political dynamics of this region. At the same time, Russia has strengthened its involvement in the Middle East, notably through its support for Syria and its relations with Iran, thereby consolidating its position as a key player in the search for solutions to regional conflicts. Finally, China's economic and political rise has also brought about substantial changes in geopolitical relations in the Middle East. In search of energy resources and economic partnerships, China has gradually extended its influence in the region, thereby altering the traditional balance of power. Competition between these global players, often played out through indirect interventions and subtle negotiations, further complicates regional issues and fuels local rivalries. Diplomatic manoeuvring, arms agreements and energy cooperation initiatives between these major powers have a direct impact on stability in the Middle East. In this context, understanding the interests and strategies of each of these actors is essential to grasping the dynamics at play and considering initiatives aimed at preserving regional peace and security.

Peace Talks: Possibilities and Deadlocks

Peace talks in the Middle East have been marked by intractable tensions, tumultuous negotiations and constantly dashed hopes. Multiple attempts to reach lasting agreements between the parties to the conflict, particularly between Iran and Israel, have faced a series of complex and deeply rooted obstacles. The thorny issue of Jerusalem's status, the fate of the occupied territories, territorial claims and the exercise of the right to self-determination have fuelled an endless cycle of unilateral talks and international mediation.

The prospects for progress towards a peaceful resolution of these conflicts have for decades appeared to be marred by structural impasses. The balance of political and military power between the parties makes any attempt at genuine compromise difficult. Any attempt at de-escalation is accompanied by inherent constraints linked to national aspirations and regional power dynamics, leading to persistent deadlocks.

Diplomatic efforts, though often motivated by laudable intentions, remain mired in the intricacies of historical antagonisms and divergent geostrategic interests. Concerted efforts to establish lasting peace are hampered by unilateral acts, provocations and military actions that continually undermine the trust necessary for any mediation process.

The impasse appears to be exacerbated by complex external factors, such as the geopolitical influences of major world powers. The ambivalent role of the United States, Russia and China in the region has often contributed to fuelling existing tensions rather than facilitating genuine peace diplomacy. The strategic agendas of external actors often interfere with local prospects for conflict resolution, creating additional obstacles.

In this context, peace talks continue to represent both a fragile hope and a complex reality. Possible ways to overcome these impasses include the need for more inclusive mediation involving a diversity of regional and international actors. Innovative initiatives focused on mutual recognition, intercultural dialogue and the restoration of the legitimate rights of affected populations could offer new avenues for progress towards building a genuine and lasting peace in the Middle East.

Impact on Civilian Populations: Humanitarian and Social

The impact of growing tensions between Iran, Israel and regional actors on civilian populations in the Middle East region is deeply rooted in the social and humanitarian fabric of these societies. The repercussions of this complex situation are felt at several levels, going well beyond diplomatic relations and political manoeuvring. On the humanitarian front, civilian populations face overwhelming challenges, particularly in terms of access to basic services such as education, healthcare and food aid. Forced displacement, loss of life and psychological trauma further exacerbate the humanitarian emergency. Society itself is undergoing deep divisions, with sectarian divisions threatening social cohesion and adversely affecting the economic fabric. Political and security instability is leading to a deterioration in living conditions, particularly affecting women, children and marginalised populations. International humanitarian organisations are therefore under unprecedented pressure to respond to the growing needs of affected populations, in a context where resources are already stretched. International solidarity is being severely tested, as humanitarian issues intertwine with complex geopolitical considerations. The humanitarian emergency requires a multidimensional response, combining immediate interventions to ensure the survival of vulnerable populations with long-term strategies to restore the resilience of affected communities. Rebuilding the social fabric, promoting social justice and preserving human rights are becoming essential imperatives in order to address the humanitarian challenges caused by regional tensions. In this context, the ability of international actors to work together in a spirit of cooperation and shared responsibility is of paramount importance in alleviating the suffering of civilian populations and preventing a prolonged humanitarian crisis.

Towards a New Regional Order: Prospects and Challenges

The turmoil in the Middle East region has long been inextricably linked to deep historical tensions, religious rivalries and struggles for geopolitical power. However, despite this complex context, it is imperative to consider the prospects for a new regional order, as well as the fundamental challenges that must be addressed. In this quest, several key elements are emerging that will shape the future of the region. First, it is important to examine the changing dynamics of relations between states and non-state actors in the Middle East. Traditional alliances are being challenged, while new coalitions are forming, redefining the balance of power. This complex evolution also raises questions about national sovereignty, collective security and regional stability. At the same time, economic and energy transitions are playing a crucial role in redefining political boundaries and strategic interests. The rise of the digital economy and innovative industries promises to transform the region's socio-economic dynamics. These upheavals also reveal major challenges in terms of social inclusion, employment and the relationship with the environment. In addition, migration and demographic issues are significantly shaping debates on national identity, urbanisation and resource management. Furthermore, territorial and border implications remain at the heart of regional issues. The redefinition of political and administrative boundaries, as well as the resolution of territorial conflicts, raise various questions about the sovereign integrity of states, inter-community coexistence and opportunities for cross-border cooperation. Finally, the issue of values, human rights and democratic governance is critical to the construction of a new regional order. The need to guarantee equality, justice and individual freedom is at the heart of citizens' aspirations and societal developments. These fundamental concerns require in-depth reflection on political structures, economic models and education systems, paving the way for a forward-looking and innovative vision for the Middle East. In conclusion, the emergence of a new regional order raises complex prospects and multidimensional challenges. By paying close and informed attention to these issues, it becomes possible to chart a course towards peace, prosperity and stability for the entire Middle East region.

References

Byman, Daniel. *Road Warriors: The Rise of the Warrior Diplomat in Mid-East Conflicts* . Oxford: Oxford University Press, 2023.

Kemp, Geoffrey, and Robert Harkavy. "Iran, Israel, and the Persian Gulf: A Delicate Equilibrium." *Survival* 63, no. 2 (2021): 7–28.

Riedel, Bruce. *Dangerous Strait: The U.S.-Iran Crisis in the Persian Gulf*. Washington, D.C.: Brookings Institution Press, 2022.

Al Jazeera. "Tensions Rise Between Iran and Israel Amid Escalating Proxy Conflicts." April 12, 2024. https://www.al-jazeera.com/news/2024/4/12/tensions-rise-between-iran-and-israel .

CHAPTER 3

Scenario 1 - Limited Conflict (2025-2026)

Immediate Economic and Geopolitical Consequences

The Eruption of Conflict: Timeline and Triggers

The current conflict can be traced back to various provocative actions by the parties involved, exacerbating tensions that were already palpable in the region. Among these triggers were a series of unannounced military manoeuvres, fuelling uncertainty and sparking a chain reaction. In addition, deep differences over the interpretation of regional agreements led to major misunderstandings, resulting in open confrontations. These displays of hostility have been greatly influenced by miscalculations, with impulsive decisions and erroneous assessments precipitating the situation towards a point of no return. A series of incidents in the months leading up to the outbreak of the conflict created a climate conducive to rising tensions, leading inevitably to violent clashes. The complexity of the underlying geopolitical issues only exacerbated the risks of a regional conflagration, jeopardising the very stability of the Middle East and beyond.

Market reaction: Oil, gas and stock indices

Geopolitical turmoil in the Middle East has always acted as a catalyst for global economic fluctuations, and the limited conflict that has erupted in the region is no exception to this rule. In the aftermath of the outbreak of the conflict, oil markets experienced unprecedented volatility, fuelled by uncertainty over future hydrocarbon supplies. Crude oil prices skyrocketed, while futures contracts came under considerable pressure, causing turmoil in investment portfolios around the world. At the same time, natural gas markets also suffered major repercussions, with prices rising significantly due to growing anxiety about the availability of gas resources. This situation had a direct impact on international stock indices, causing turmoil in global financial markets. Investors faced a period of imminent economic instability, frantically seeking to assess the risks associated with companies operating in the energy sector. The strategic decisions taken by major financial institutions proved crucial, shaping the trends observed on the stock markets. Initial reactions to events in the Middle East led to intense trading, marked by speculative movements and rapid adjustments to asset portfolios. The international community was kept on tenterhooks by these developments, aware of their potential impact on the global economy. In this climate of nervousness, markets fluctuated in response to official statements, rumours and macroeconomic indicators, reflecting the high level of uncertainty prevailing in financial circles. As stock market operators engaged in a complex dance in a constantly changing environment, governments and central banks had to intervene to mitigate the adverse effects of the crisis, attempting to restore investor confidence and ensure global financial stability.

The Impact on Global Trade Routes: Suez and Bab el-Mandeb

The limited conflict in the Strait of Hormuz sent shockwaves around the world, with a particularly significant impact on the crucial trade routes of Suez and Bab el-Mandeb. These vital waterways, through which a significant portion of global maritime trade passes, were deeply affected by the geopolitical tensions caused by the conflict.

The disruption of trade flows through the Suez Canal, linking the Mediterranean Sea to the Red Sea, has caused serious concern within the international community. With thousands of merchant ships carrying various cargoes, any disruption to transit through the canal has major economic repercussions. Delays in the delivery of goods, higher transport costs and supply chain instability are all challenges facing global economic players.

On the other hand, the situation in the Bab el-Mandeb Strait, a strategic passage between the Red Sea and the Indian Ocean, is also causing significant concern. Any disruption in this key region would have a direct impact on international maritime trade by altering shipping routes and exposing vessels to new security risks. Soaring marine insurance premiums, increased operating costs and the need to redefine security protocols are just some of the immediate consequences of this geopolitical instability.

In short, the impact on global trade routes, particularly through Suez and Bab el-Mandeb, is a crucial factor to consider when assessing the potential damage caused by the limited conflict in the Strait of Hormuz. This reality highlights the deep interconnection between regional geopolitical events and global economic dynamics, and underscores the inherent vulnerability of the global economy to major geopolitical crises.

Alliances in Flux: Strategic Pivoting of International Powers

The inevitable conflict in the Strait of Hormuz has triggered a major realignment of geopolitical alliances worldwide. Traditional and emerging powers have been forced to revisit their strategic partnerships to address the challenges posed by the crisis. The European Union, historically dependent on oil and gas from the region, has sought to diversify its energy supply sources, implementing ambitious plans to increase its resilience to market disruptions. At the same time, Russia and China have strengthened their economic and military cooperation, consolidating their position in the Middle East region. Tensions between the United States and Iran have also catalysed a rapprochement between Washington and some Gulf countries, redrawing the balance of power in the region. In Africa, coastal countries have stepped up efforts to secure their maritime routes and protect their economic interests amid increased competition. This strategic pivot by international powers has not only redefined the boundaries of geopolitical influence, but has also shaped new dynamics of cooperation and rivalry on a global scale. The Strait of Hormuz has become the focal point around which the aspirations and ambitions of international actors are crystallising, with major repercussions for the global geopolitical balance.

Military Operations: Deployments and Tactical Issues

The evolution of military operations in the context of the limited conflict in 2025-2026 has prompted close scrutiny from geopolitical analysts and international observers. The strategic deployments of the armed forces of the actors involved have not only redrawn tactical boundaries, but have also multiplied security challenges at the regional and global levels. The emergence of innovative technologies such as autonomous drones and hypersonic missiles has profoundly changed the nature of confrontations, creating new challenges for the application of international humanitarian law. Competition for control of critical sea lanes has become a focal point, leading to high-intensity naval confrontations and manoeuvres aimed at securing energy supply lines. At the same time, ground forces have conducted intelligence operations and targeted missions to weaken adversary capabilities, while navigating a complex context of asymmetric warfare. The selective use of cyber and information operations has also been highlighted, revealing the growing importance of the digital domain in the conduct of hostilities. At the tactical level, the preservation of strategic infrastructure such as oil and gas facilities has been at the heart of operational priorities, with major implications for the economic resilience of the states concerned. Ethical dilemmas related to the protection of civilian populations in a complex combat environment have generated intense debate within the decision-making bodies of the armed forces. In this new age of conflict, understanding operational dynamics is crucial to grasping the strategic implications of the ongoing conflict.

Crisis Diplomacy: Disarmament Initiatives and Negotiations

The period following the outbreak of a conflict is crucial for international diplomacy. While military operations reshape the tactical landscape, diplomatic actors scramble to defuse the crisis. Disarmament initiatives, secret negotiations and international mediation come into play in a complex ballet where every move can tip the balance between peace and chaos.

The world's major powers find themselves at the heart of this theatre of crisis diplomacy. Behind the scenes of international relations, intense diplomatic activity is underway, with high-level emissaries conducting confidential talks aimed at establishing channels of communication and exploring ways out of the crisis. Tensions are palpable, with every decision weighing heavily on the precarious balance between the actors involved.

At the same time, international organisations such as the UN and the European Union are working to promote de-escalation initiatives and facilitate constructive negotiations. Mediation and peaceful conflict resolution mechanisms are being called upon, creating a space conducive to the search for consensual solutions.

In this tense atmosphere, political, economic and human issues are intertwined.

Crisis diplomacy requires finesse and perseverance, as the divergent interests of the parties involved make any potential agreement subject to complex negotiations. Ideological and strategic differences can complicate talks, prolonging uncertainty and instability. Ultimately, crisis diplomacy reflects the race against time to prevent widespread conflict.

Every disarmament initiative and every step forward in negotiations represents a step towards the peaceful resolution of the conflict. International cooperation, despite its challenges, remains vital to finding sustainable solutions to these periods of crisis. The ability of diplomatic actors to transcend divisions and foster dialogue remains essential to preserving global security and the integrity of populations affected by conflict.

Humanitarian Consequences: Refugee Influx and International Aid

The escalation of the conflict in the region has led to an unprecedented humanitarian crisis, marked by a massive influx of refugees fleeing the combat zones. Precarious living conditions in refugee camps have exacerbated the suffering of displaced populations, straining the reception capacities of neighbouring countries. At the same time, the international community has mobilised to provide urgent humanitarian aid, but the scale of the needs far exceeds the resources available. Humanitarian agencies, already facing multiple crises around the world, are struggling to respond to this new emergency, and calls for global solidarity have been issued.

In this critical situation, it is imperative that international actors coordinate their efforts to ensure effective assistance to populations in distress. Cooperation between humanitarian organisations, governments and local actors is crucial to alleviate suffering and prevent a major humanitarian disaster. To guarantee respect for the fundamental rights of refugees, it is essential to establish adequate protection mechanisms and promote sustainable solutions, including through resettlement and reintegration programmes.

At the same time, it is important to emphasise the importance of supporting host countries facing increasing pressure due to the influx of refugees. These nations, often already facing their own economic and social challenges, deserve significant support from the international community to address this complex situation. Financial, technical and logistical assistance must be implemented in a coordinated manner, taking into account the cultural and social specificities of host communities.

Ultimately, the humanitarian dimension of this conflict requires a concerted and resolute response, based on the fundamental principles of human dignity, solidarity and shared responsibility. Managing this crisis requires sustained commitment from all actors involved, in order to protect vulnerable lives and preserve hope for a better future for those who have been displaced by the ravages of war.

The Dynamics of Sanctions: Economic Pressure and Regional Repercussions

The application of economic sanctions in the context of a limited conflict such as the one raging around the Strait of Hormuz is a complex process with far-reaching consequences. Economic pressure is intended to change the behaviour of the actors involved in the conflict, but it also has often unpredictable regional repercussions.

Sanctions generally take various forms, ranging from targeted trade restrictions to complete bans on imports and exports. In this case, the strategic nature of the strait makes it a focal point for coercive action. The international actors involved seek to exert pressure on the parties involved in order to influence the course of the conflict and promote a peaceful resolution.

However, the regional repercussions of sanctions are manifold. The economic impact extends far beyond the immediate borders of the conflict zone, affecting the energy, maritime trade and finance sectors. Oil and gas suppliers and buyers are facing major disruptions, while logistics operators are experiencing unprecedented constraints on their activities.

Furthermore, the effects of sanctions are also being felt on regional political and security dynamics. Increased pressure may lead to unexpected strategic realignments, threatening the already precarious balance in certain geopolitical areas. Neighbouring states are particularly vulnerable to the fallout from restrictive measures, and the stability of the entire region is being tested.

Finally, the human aspects of economic sanctions must be examined. Local populations may suffer shortages and difficulties in accessing basic necessities, raising ethical questions about the impact of international actions on innocent citizens. Humanitarian aid then becomes crucial in alleviating the suffering caused by coercive measures.

Far from being linear, the dynamics of sanctions thus generate profound ramifications that go beyond the simple economic framework. The study of these repercussions is an essential pillar of contemporary geopolitical analysis and fuels debates on the most effective means of managing international crises while respecting the rights and dignity of peoples.

Public Perceptions: Media, Information Warfare and International Opinion

Public perceptions play a crucial role in the management of international crises. In a limited conflict such as the one envisaged in the scenario presented, the media and information warfare become key players. On the one hand, traditional media and digital platforms often amplify and distort the reality on the ground. Shocking images, poignant testimonies and partisan analysis all contribute to shaping public opinion through the prism of emotion and bias. On the other hand, information warfare takes on a major strategic dimension. Military leaders, intelligence agencies and non-state organisations clash in the media to influence perceptions and legitimise their actions. The spread of fake news, the manipulation of social media and the demonisation of opponents are commonplace. Faced with this profusion of information and disinformation, international opinion is often confused. It is therefore imperative to take a critical look at media discourse and exercise a keen analytical mind in order to avoid falling into the trap of propaganda. Paradoxically, the over-abundance of information can also lead to a form of information fatigue, where the public gradually turns away from the media and retreats to more limited sources of information. This then creates risks of polarisation and intellectual isolation. Thus, communication and public perception issues weigh heavily on the evolution of conflicts and possible ways out. An in-depth analysis of these phenomena is necessary to fully understand contemporary geopolitical dynamics.

Future scenarios: Probabilities of de-escalation or escalation

The question of future scenarios in the face of a limited conflict such as the one envisaged in this analysis gives rise to multiple hypotheses and conjectures. The probabilities of de-escalation or escalation are based on a constellation of complex factors, intertwined with international relations and the socio-political dynamics of regional actors. First, it is necessary to examine the diplomatic efforts underway to initiate a process of de-escalation. The interactions between the main mediators, the possible intervention of the international community, and the channels of negotiation between the warring parties are crucial in assessing the prospects for de-escalation. The analysis also takes into account the ability of the actors involved to absorb the economic, political and human costs of maintaining the conflict.

The resilience of regional alliances and the willingness of global powers to influence the search for a peaceful solution will largely determine the future trajectory of the conflict. However, unpredictable factors such as unintended military incidents, terrorist acts or internal pressures can suddenly lead to unexpected escalation. Assessing the risks of this scenario therefore requires a detailed analysis of potential hazards and possible flaws in any process to control hostilities. With this in mind, it is crucial to examine the strategic options available to each actor involved in the crisis in order to anticipate possible choices in the event of a deadlock or an opportunity to end the crisis. Finally, the mobilisation of civil society, humanitarian organisations and independent experts can play a significant role in creating an environment conducive to the search for concerted solutions. These factors determine the complexity of future scenarios, where each sequence of events and each reaction by the actors will have a decisive influence on the spiral of escalation or the opening towards a peaceful outcome.

References

Gholz, Eugene. "Limited War and Energy Markets: Assessing Short-Term Disruptions." *Security Studies* 31, no. 4 (2022): 678–701.

RAND Corporation. *Regional Conflict and Economic Spillovers: Scenarios for the Middle East* . Santa Monica, CA: RAND Corporation, 2022. https://www.rand.org/pubs/research_reports/RRA193-1.html .

World Bank. *Global Economic Prospects: Regional Risks and Resilience* . Washington, D.C.: World Bank Publications, 2023.

CHAPTER 4

The consequences for the main regional players

Saudi Arabia, the United Arab Emirates and Iran

The Arab-Persian Gulf under pressure

The Arab-Persian Gulf remains a major theatre of international geopolitics, where fragile balances are subject to multiple pressures. Geopolitical upheavals, exacerbated by military and economic tensions, require an in-depth analysis of the security, economic and diplomatic issues weighing on the region. At the heart of this instability, Saudi Arabia, the United Arab Emirates and Iran face unprecedented challenges. Geostrategic issues, regional rivalry and internal political upheaval are converging to create a climate of great uncertainty. Saudi Arabia, a bastion of political conservatism, is facing profound changes both at home and abroad. Power consolidation, economic reforms and diplomatic initiatives are testing the stability of the Wahhabi kingdom in the face of Iranian ambitions and a region in turmoil. For its part, the United Arab Emirates, another major player in the global economy, is taking an ambitious and proactive stance. However, security challenges in a context of heightened tensions with Iran and pressure from regional conflicts raise serious questions about the sustainability of its growing influence. As for Iran, it faces unprecedented economic and geopolitical pressures. International sanctions and regional rivalries are contributing to a redefinition of its strategies and alliances, while fuelling tensions in the region. Thus, these major players in the Arab-Persian Gulf are subject to complex dynamics that threaten the fragile balance of the region and have considerable global implications. It is imperative to carefully analyse these interconnections in order to understand the consequences of these heightened geopolitical pressures.

Saudi Arabia: Internal political changes and challenges to stability

For several years, Saudi Arabia has been undergoing a series of major political changes, guided by Crown Prince Mohammed bin Salman's Vision 2030. This initiative aims to diversify the Saudi economy and reduce its dependence on oil revenues. However, these reforms face many challenges, both internally and externally.

Internally, the reforms are accompanied by a questioning of traditional power structures. The political and economic elites, accustomed to a certain status quo, are seeing the emergence of new dynamics that are causing tensions and resistance. In addition, Saudi Arabia's youth, who make up a large proportion of the population, have growing expectations in terms of employment, education and individual freedoms, putting additional pressure on the reform process.

At the same time, on the regional stage, Saudi Arabia faces major security challenges, including the rise of Iranian influence in the region and the ongoing conflicts in Yemen and Syria. These external factors complicate the Saudi kingdom's efforts to transform itself internally and stabilise its economy.

In addition, the transition to a diversified, knowledge-based economy requires profound adjustments to both the labour market and infrastructure. Implementing these reforms will require careful management of political and social balances in order to avoid divisions within Saudi society.

Faced with these challenges, Saudi Arabia is engaged in a delicate exercise of consolidating political power, modernising the economy and preserving regional stability. How the Saudi kingdom navigates this tumultuous period will have significant repercussions for the future of the Gulf and the regional geopolitical balance.

Vision 2030 in the face of geopolitical realities

In a changing geopolitical context, Saudi Arabia has embarked on an unprecedented societal and economic transformation with Vision 2030. This ambitious initiative aims to diversify the kingdom's economy, reduce its dependence on oil, and modernise its institutions. However, this reform effort faces multiple challenges, particularly on the geopolitical front. As the country seeks to position itself as a key global player, it must navigate skilfully amid regional rivalries and international tensions. Vision 2030 is an integral part of Saudi Arabia's overall strategy to ensure its national security and maintain its influence in a volatile Middle East where traditional balances are being disrupted. Domestically, the reform process is sparking debate and resistance, with the authorities having to reconcile modernisation with the preservation of traditions. Internationally, the implementation of Vision 2030 requires shrewd diplomacy to establish Saudi legitimacy and forge strategic alliances. In addition, bilateral relations with major players such as the United States, China and Russia will also determine the success of Saudi Arabia's ambitions. Furthermore, regional dynamics, notably the conflict in Yemen, tensions with Iran and the Gulf crisis, are putting considerable pressure on Saudi Arabia's ability to implement its vision for the future. Vision 2030 therefore reflects the Kingdom's desire to adapt to the new precepts of global geopolitics while preserving its cultural and religious identity. Its outcome will determine not only the fate of Saudi Arabia, but also the balance of power in the Middle East and beyond.

United Arab Emirates: From logistics hub to diplomatic player

The United Arab Emirates (UAE), heir to a history marked by its role as a commercial transit point and logistics hub, has undergone a rapid transformation to become a key diplomatic player on the international stage. This change has been driven by a bold vision that has enabled the UAE to diversify its economy and extend its political influence beyond its borders.

In the early decades of the 21st century, the UAE rethought its geostrategic positioning, taking advantage of its privileged geographical location at the crossroads of Europe, Africa and Asia. With massive investment and innovative infrastructure, the Emirates have established a major commercial hub, attracting flows of goods and capital to their ports and free zones. This transformation has been accompanied by a policy of economic diversification aimed at reducing the country's dependence on crude oil, the traditional pillar of its economy.

In parallel with this economic reorientation, the UAE has capitalised on its status as a place of intercultural encounter and thriving trade to initiate an ambitious foreign policy. It has been actively involved in mediating regional conflicts and has cultivated strategic alliances with various world powers. Its pragmatic and proactive diplomacy has also earned it a prominent place in international trade negotiations. By positioning itself as a credible voice in multilateral forums, particularly within the UN, the UAE has signalled its willingness to contribute to the resolution of global issues while defending its national interests.

The rise of the UAE on the international stage has reconfigured the geopolitical balance in the Middle East. Its influence now extends beyond the economic sphere to the political and socio-cultural spheres. However, this evolution also calls for a critical analysis of the potential repercussions, whether in terms of security risks linked to its position as a mediator or possible tensions with regional actors with divergent interests. The UAE's rise from a logistics hub to a leading diplomatic player raises exciting and complex issues that deserve close attention from observers and geopolitical analysts.

Abu Dhabi faces security and economic challenges

Abu Dhabi, the capital of the United Arab Emirates, finds itself at the crossroads of many security and economic issues that shape regional dynamics. In terms of security, its geographical proximity to Iran and the ongoing tensions in the Strait of Hormuz place the city at the heart of challenges related to regional stability. The need to ensure the security of vital shipping lanes for global trade gives Abu Dhabi a crucial role in security cooperation with its international partners. At the same time, the fight against terrorism and extremism requires constant vigilance, reinforcing the need for a coherent and proactive security policy. On the economic front, diversifying investment sectors and seeking energy independence are major priorities for Abu Dhabi. The United Arab Emirates' Vision 2030 aims to increase the resilience of the national economy, in particular by reducing historical dependence on oil and promoting the development of sectors such as renewable energy, technology and tourism. However, global market volatility and oil price fluctuations are constant challenges to the implementation of this vision. Faced with these challenges, Abu Dhabi is asserting itself as a key regional player, combining active diplomacy, strategic investments and international alliances to secure its position in a rapidly changing Middle East. Striking a balance between security considerations and economic imperatives is therefore a key challenge for the foreign and domestic policy of the Emirati capital, which is called upon to play an essential role in building a stable and prosperous future for the region.

Iran: Economic resilience and a new regional strategy

Despite international economic pressure and severe sanctions, Iran has demonstrated remarkable economic resilience in recent years. In response to the challenges posed by trade restrictions, Tehran has diversified its economy by focusing on non-oil sectors such as information technology, healthcare, tourism and other emerging industries. This strategy has enabled Iran to reduce its excessive dependence on oil and stimulate economic growth in more sustainable areas.

At the same time, Iran has adopted a new regional strategy aimed at strengthening its alliances with various regional actors, particularly allied militias that share its geopolitical interests. Iran's growing influence in the Middle East, particularly in countries such as Iraq, Syria, and Lebanon, reflects its determination to shape the region's political dynamics in order to consolidate its strategic position. This strategy is also accompanied by an amplification of Shiite influence, providing Tehran with a solid base from which to expand its political and security footprint.

However, this regional expansion is not without controversy, raising concerns among some regional and international powers. Regional rivalry between Iran and Saudi Arabia, as well as ongoing tensions with Israel, are fuelling concerns about the shifting balance of power in the Middle East. Recent attacks attributed to Iran or Iran-backed groups have intensified these fears and contributed to a climate of regional mistrust and uncertainty.

In this complex context, Iran seeks to assert its sovereignty and protect its national interests while preserving its regional alliances and strengthening its ability to shape the geopolitical agenda. Iran's ability to navigate these internal and external challenges will continue to play a central role in the geopolitical dynamics of the Middle East and beyond.

The Role of Allied Militias and Shiite Influence in the Region

The influence of allied militias and the rise of Shiism as a geopolitical force are crucial elements in the complex dynamics shaping the Middle East region. Allied militias, often backed by Iran, have significantly altered the traditional balance of power in the Middle East, thereby consolidating Tehran's influence in the region. This non-state military presence has created major challenges for state actors, particularly Saudi Arabia and the United Arab Emirates, which are striving to counter this territorial and ideological expansion. The consolidation of allied militia networks in Iraq, Syria, Lebanon and Yemen has also contributed to redrawing the map of regional alliances and increasing the complexity of intra-state tensions. At the same time, the rise of Shiite influence in the region has led to significant geopolitical upheavals. Shiism, long marginalised on the regional stage, has gradually emerged as a notable political, diplomatic and military force. The intensification of relations between Iran and certain Shiite political actors and militias has consolidated the religious and political influence of this branch of Islam in countries such as Iraq, Lebanon and Yemen, prompting a series of contrasting reactions among the dominant Sunni actors in the region. These developments have led to increased sectarian polarisation, exacerbating tensions and having major repercussions on regional conflicts and power balances, with direct implications for mediation and negotiation processes. Thus, careful analysis of the role of allied militias and Shiite influence in the region is crucial to understanding the tangible geopolitical dynamics that transcend traditional state borders and profoundly influence the evolution of power relations in the Middle East.

Alliance and rivalry: Dynamics between Riyadh and Tehran

Relations between Saudi Arabia and Iran, the two predominant regional players in the Middle East, are marked by a long history of rivalries and shifting alliances. These two powers have diametrically opposed visions for the region, highlighting complex and often conflicting dynamics. The history of relations between these two regional giants is marked by political, religious and economic competition, frequently resulting in tensions and open confrontation.

The rivalry between Riyadh and Tehran stems in particular from deep religious differences, with Saudi Arabia as the self-proclaimed guardian of Sunni Islam's holy sites and Iran representing the world's largest Shia population. This ideological confrontation has gradually evolved into a struggle for regional influence, with destabilising implications for the entire region. The diplomatic positions of Saudi Arabia and Iran diverge on a wide range of issues, fuelling a bitter rivalry with no immediate hope of resolution.

Recent episodes such as the war in Yemen, unrest in Iraq, conflicts in Syria, and instability in Lebanon have reinforced the image of a hegemonic struggle between these two regional powers. Their competing activities in these countries have exacerbated sectarian and political divisions, helping to fuel conflicts throughout the region.

However, despite this intense rivalry, both actors have also been involved in occasional attempts at dialogue and cooperation. Efforts at appeasement have been observed at various times, particularly during regional crises. This raises questions about the volatile nature of their relationship, which oscillates between confrontation and détente, offering a fascinating insight into the complexities of international relations.

In short, the alliance and rivalry between Riyadh and Tehran continue to leave an indelible mark on the geopolitical theatre of the Middle East, reflecting crucial issues that shape the future of the region and beyond. Understanding these complex dynamics is essential to grasping the security and political challenges posed by this formidable interaction between two powers with considerable regional ambitions.

Diplomatic Efforts by Regional Actors with Global Powers

The fragile balance in the Middle East is prompting regional actors such as Saudi Arabia, the United Arab Emirates and Iran to undertake strenuous diplomatic efforts to influence global powers. These complex interactions shape a constantly changing geopolitical landscape, where alliances are forged and broken in the quest for international support.

Saudi Arabia, aware of its regional preponderance, is engaged in proactive diplomacy with the major Western powers. The Saudi kingdom seeks to ensure the maintenance of its strategic alliances while exerting influence on crucial international decisions. Recent geopolitical developments have led to an increased emphasis on diversifying diplomatic relations, reflecting a desire to strengthen Saudi Arabia's position on the world stage in a period of growing uncertainty.

Similarly, the United Arab Emirates, a veritable economic and military crossroads, is deploying multifaceted diplomacy aimed at extending its influence on the world stage. Through strategic trade alliances and major investments, the Emirates are seeking to shape an environment conducive to their regional vision, while cultivating privileged relations with key players such as the United States and the European Union. This subtle approach marks a gradual transition towards proactive diplomacy aimed at consolidating the Emirates' position on the world stage.

In contrast, Iran, facing economic and political challenges amid growing international pressure, is relying on a diplomacy of resistance to mobilise international support against its adversaries. The focus is on strengthening ties with regional and global actors that share common interests, while Iran skilfully exploits the nuances of contemporary diplomacy to counterbalance initiatives that run counter to its national interests.

These diplomatic efforts by regional actors are undoubtedly shaping the dynamics of international relations. They reflect a complex struggle for influence and legitimacy, which, rooted in deeply intertwined regional realities, gives the Middle East region a crucial role in the evolution of the global order. In this subtle diplomatic game, regional actors are mobilising their strategic assets in a frantic quest for security and supremacy, thereby contributing to the redrawing of international geopolitical boundaries.

Conclusion: Towards a redefinition of the balance of power in the Middle East

The Middle East has entered an era of unprecedented geopolitical upheaval, creating a climate of uncertainty and transformation. Regional actors, notably Saudi Arabia, the United Arab Emirates and Iran, face multidimensional challenges that are redefining the power dynamics in this region crucial to global stability.

Over the past few decades, these actors have sought to consolidate their regional position by developing strategies to increase their political, economic and security influence. However, the emergence of new actors and new challenges has disrupted this fragile balance. Tensions between Riyadh and Tehran, internal political upheavals in Saudi Arabia and the regional ambitions of the United Arab Emirates reflect a constantly changing dynamic.

The redefinition of power relations in the Middle East also revolves around complex interactions with global powers. Relations with the United States, Russia, China and the European Union significantly influence the decisions and strategic orientations of regional actors. These global powers seek to exploit divisions and rivalries between regional actors to achieve their own geopolitical objectives, further complicating the regional landscape.

The rise of allied militias in Iran and the growing involvement of the United Arab Emirates in regional affairs are contributing to heightened competition, jeopardising the region's already fragile stability. Furthermore, the repercussions of the conflicts in Syria, Yemen and Iraq continue to weigh heavily on power dynamics, exacerbating existing rivalries.

Faced with these challenges, a redefinition of the balance of power in the Middle East seems inevitable. Regional actors will need to rebuild alliances, re-evaluate strategies, and seek diplomatic solutions to prevent escalating tensions and widespread regional destabilisation. This redefinition will also offer opportunities for constructive cooperation to address common challenges such as energy security, counter-terrorism, and humanitarian crisis management.

In conclusion, the redefinition of power relations in the Middle East will require a balanced approach based on dialogue, diplomacy and mutual respect for legitimate interests. This complex process will need to take into account regional aspirations while promoting stability and prosperity for all countries in the region and for the international community.

References

House, Karen Elliott. *Saudi Arabia and the New Middle East Order*. New York: Knopf, 2023.

Henderson, Simon. "The UAE's Strategic Shift: Hedging Between Washington and Tehran." *The Washington Institute for Near East Policy*, Policy Focus No. 179, 2024.

Cordesman, Anthony H. *Iranian Power: Past, Present, and Future*. Westport, CT: Greenwood Publishing Group, 2022.

CHAPTER 5

Scenario 2 - Prolonged Partial Disruption

(2026-2028) An Energy Crisis Looms

Historical Context: Towards a New Energy Normal

Over the decades, major disruptions in the energy market have shaped nations' attitudes and policies towards energy supply. The oil crises of the 1970s sent shockwaves around the world, changing perceptions of the finite nature of energy reserves and excessive dependence on specific sources. These historic events continue to exert a profound influence on current strategic choices as countries strive to prevent a repeat of past crises. The collective memory of energy shortages and sharp price increases remains embedded in national policies, guiding actions to enhance energy security.

The search for diversification of supply sources and transport routes has been a central element of strategies to mitigate the impact of any potential disruptive events. Lessons learned from periods of geopolitical tension, conflict or unexpected changes in energy markets have prompted many international actors to rethink their national energy policies and promote greater co-operation between nations. However, despite these attempts to prevent future disruptions, contemporary challenges such as climate change, rising economic nationalism and increased competition for access to resources are testing the ability of states to maintain long-term energy stability.

Thus, the historical perspective reminds us that even when nations strive to anticipate and prevent energy disruptions, the complex evolution of geopolitical dynamics and national aspirations can make the transition to a new energy normal difficult. In this constantly changing environment, in-depth analysis of the historical context is essential to understanding current expectations regarding energy supply and to forging appropriate policies to meet future challenges.

Geopolitical Challenge: National Rivals and Strategic Alliances

In a world where energy resources have become the central pivot of international relations, national rivalries are becoming increasingly acute. Traditional poles of influence such as the United States, Russia, China and the European Union are facing an unprecedented transformation of the geostrategic balance. The issue of access to and control of energy resources is therefore becoming an absolute priority, determining not only strategic alliances but also potential regional and global conflicts. This race for energy power is accompanied by active diplomacy, with bilateral treaties and multilateral agreements constantly redrawing the geopolitical landscape.

Short-term economic impact: from inflation to recession

The prolonged disruption of global energy flows has profound and immediate economic repercussions. Rising energy prices, particularly for fuels, are being felt across all sectors of the economy. These higher production costs are being passed on to consumers, who are seeing their purchasing power decline. Businesses are also under increasing pressure, which is making it difficult for them to remain profitable. In addition, countries heavily dependent on energy imports are facing increased trade deficits, further exacerbating their economic vulnerabilities. Faced with these inflationary pressures, monetary authorities are being forced to review their policies, risking financial and monetary stability. This difficult economic situation could quickly slide into recession if no decisive action is taken. Structural imbalances and a loss of confidence among economic actors could plunge the global economy into a downward spiral. It is therefore imperative that governments and international institutions put in place effective measures to stem these harmful effects. The ability of political and economic actors to navigate this turbulent period with caution and vision will largely determine the future trajectory of the global economy.

The Evocation of Sanctions: The Economic Weapon at the Heart of Diplomatic Gamesmanship

Against a backdrop of prolonged partial disruption to global energy supplies, state powers are turning to the economic weapon of sanctions to protect their strategic interests. Economic sanctions have become a key tool, and sometimes the last resort, in international diplomatic gamesmanship. Their reach extends far beyond national borders, affecting not only the targeted economy but also global political relations. When a major player deploys economic sanctions, the repercussions can be felt worldwide.

Sanctions increase pressure on targeted actors, forcing them to weigh the economic and political costs of their actions. However, the effects of economic sanctions can be complex and unpredictable. Although designed to inflict economic damage, they can also strengthen the resilience of targeted regimes by encouraging greater autonomy and alternative partnerships. Furthermore, sanctions can generate additional tensions between international actors, creating further challenges for diplomacy.

Faced with an impending energy crisis, world powers must decide on the path forward with regard to economic sanctions. International coordination is crucial to avoid a spiral of retaliation and restrictive countermeasures, which would only intensify the crisis. Countries should consider joint diplomatic measures to ensure economic and geopolitical stability in the context of prolonged energy disruption. In the context of such instability, the usefulness of sanctions must be carefully considered, with particular attention paid to the possible domestic and international consequences. Ultimately, the use of economic sanctions in the context of an energy crisis should be accompanied by constant dialogue and close collaboration between international actors in order to prevent harmful escalation and promote sustainable solutions.

International Response: Coordination or Competition?

The prolonged disruption of energy flows is creating a crucial dilemma for the international community. Faced with this looming energy crisis, the nations of the world find themselves at a strategic crossroads, with divergent choices between harmonious multilateral coordination and heightened competition for access to remaining resources. This dichotomy raises fundamental issues of energy security, geopolitical stability and economic equity. While some advocate cooperation and mutual interdependence as viable solutions, others favour protectionist and unilateral policies. The central question therefore remains: how can states respond to this crisis in a way that preserves the integrity of the global energy system while safeguarding their national interests?

In this delicate context, we are seeing the emergence of coalitions and informal alliances aimed either at pooling available resources or strengthening their relative position in the new global energy hierarchy. Negotiations are intensifying around mechanisms for equitable sharing, financial compensation and bilateral or regional commitments. At the same time, traditional rivalries are intensifying, leading to a frantic race to secure supplies, while the spectre of potential conflict looms over certain key regions.

International institutions such as the UN, the European Union and OPEC are faced with a major imperative to redefine their roles and mandates. There is heated debate about the ability of these bodies to act proactively and effectively in such a turbulent environment. The effectiveness of mediation and preventive diplomacy mechanisms is being severely tested, as pressure mounts to find sustainable solutions that are acceptable to all.

Beyond state borders, a diverse array of non-state actors is reshaping the geopolitical landscape, from smugglers and shadowy groups to transnational entities operating in cyberspace. These entities are exerting growing influence, challenging regulators and shifting the balance of power in unpredictable ways. The confrontation between the traditional order and new forms of power therefore poses a major challenge to the established international order.

Faced with this complex landscape, the search for viable solutions requires bold vision and unwavering collective will. Only a clever combination of diplomatic pragmatism and constructive solidarity can offer hope for stabilisation while avoiding the pitfalls of uncontrolled escalation. As tensions intensify and divergent interests sharpen, the path to an optimal international response remains fraught with obstacles and uncertain compromises.

Non-State Actors: From the Black Market to Cyberspace

The large-scale energy crisis looming between 2026 and 2028 does not only concern states and international alliances. Indeed, another fundamental aspect of this situation lies in the involvement of non-state actors, who are evolving from the traditional black market to cyberspace. These entities may include rebel groups, criminal organisations, and even private actors seeking to profit from the situation. In the context of prolonged disruption to energy flows, these non-state actors may play a decisive role in the parallel economy, maritime security, and information warfare. The energy black market, already present in some unstable regions, could expand and put additional pressure on national authorities and legitimate economic actors. Similarly, modern piracy, whether motivated by economic or geopolitical interests, poses a serious threat to maritime security, with potentially destabilising consequences for global trade. Furthermore, cyberspace has become a virtual battlefield where attacks on energy infrastructure and control systems are a growing concern. Non-state actors exploit vulnerabilities in digital connectivity to influence and disrupt energy supply chains, posing major challenges for security and resilience. Furthermore, the spread of false information and manipulated narratives can influence public opinion and exacerbate social and political tensions. In this complex context, the interaction between non-state actors and state and international dynamics is becoming a crucial issue for global stability. It is imperative to understand and anticipate the strategies of these actors in order to develop effective and coherent responses to protect common interests in a volatile and contested energy environment.

Maritime Security: The Spectre of Modern Piracy

Strategic sea lanes, once the theatre of confrontation between major powers, now face an insidious and shifting threat: modern piracy. From crucial straits to vital trade routes, no maritime area is immune to this worrying resurgence. While the romanticised image of pirates may raise a smile, the reality of these criminal acts is very different. Modern piracy, characterised by its transnational nature and increasing sophistication, represents a serious challenge to global maritime security. Organised gangs operating on the high seas are no longer content with simple acts of theft, but also threaten the lives of crews and the stability of trade. From West Africa to Southeast Asia, the seas are the scene of a complex struggle between law enforcement agencies and these agile criminal groups. The international response to this threat cannot be limited to unilateral initiatives. It requires effective multilateral coordination, enhanced regional cooperation, and rigorous implementation of international conventions. Furthermore, the technological dimension of this battle at sea is crucial. From advanced surveillance systems to secure communication protocols, technological innovation plays an essential role in protecting maritime routes. Nevertheless, the challenges posed by modern piracy are not limited to the material sphere. They extend to the legal domain, where the definition of maritime crimes and the prosecution of perpetrators require sustained attention. Beyond tactical considerations, this fight calls for a deep understanding of the socio-economic and political factors that contribute to the emergence of modern piracy. Social injustice, poverty, and political instability can provide fertile ground for these illegal activities. Thus, maritime security cannot be addressed in isolation from global development and governance issues. Faced with this spectre of modern piracy, it is imperative to create a united front, transcending state borders, in order to protect essential sea lanes and ensure the stability of global trade.

Technological Innovation: Adaptation and Resilience in Times of Uncertainty

Technological innovation, often overshadowed by geopolitical and economic narratives, plays a critical role in the ability of nations to adapt and prosper in times of energy uncertainty. Adapting to prolonged disruptions in the energy market requires significant advances in various technological fields. Among these, progress in renewable energy and storage technologies is of paramount importance.

Against the backdrop of an energy crisis, massive investments in renewable energy offer a ray of hope. Rapid advances in solar, wind and hydroelectric technologies have significantly reduced the cost of clean energy production, making these alternatives more economically attractive. At the same time, the development of advanced storage solutions, such as high-capacity batteries and thermal storage systems, is helping to overcome the inherent intermittency of renewable energies, thereby ensuring a more stable energy supply.

Beyond traditional energy sources, advances in carbon capture and storage (CCS) technologies also offer significant potential for mitigating environmental impacts while maintaining an adequate energy supply. By combining the capture of CO_2 emitted by industrial facilities with its long-term underground storage, CCS systems pave the way for a more sustainable use of existing fossil resources. These developments require continued investment in research and development, as well as increased international cooperation to share knowledge and best practices.

In addition, advances in digitalisation and connectivity offer significant opportunities to optimise energy efficiency, reduce transmission losses and promote smarter energy network management. Artificial intelligence, the Internet of Things (IoT) and smart grid solutions create opportunities for real-time optimisation, promoting more efficient use of energy resources and greater operational resilience to external shocks. However, these technological advances also bring cybersecurity challenges, requiring increased vigilance and international cooperation to mitigate potential risks.

Ultimately, technological innovation is not only a means of mitigating the adverse effects of a prolonged energy crisis, but also embodies a source of new and promising opportunities. The urgent need for adaptation and resilience in times of uncertainty is ushering in a new era of technological progress, shaping not only the energy transition but also the very evolution of global geopolitical and economic dynamics.

Domestic Scene: New Social and Political Dynamics

The geopolitical tensions and energy disruptions in this scenario are not limited to a simple global economic crisis. They are also triggering profound upheavals in the social and political dynamics within states. Indeed, the scarcity of energy resources and the resulting inflationary pressure are having a direct impact on the daily lives of citizens, triggering chain reactions within each society. Social inequalities are widening, creating a sense of injustice and frustration among populations already weakened by years of recurring economic crises. This precarious situation is giving rise to social protest movements, some peaceful but others more radical, threatening the internal stability of states. At the same time, internal political dynamics are also being disrupted. Governments are facing increasing pressure to meet the urgent needs of their populations while juggling the geostrategic imperatives imposed by the energy crisis. Political realignments are taking shape, with some authoritarian regimes strengthening their grip in the face of growing opposition, while fragile democracies are seeing their legitimacy challenged by disenchanted populations. Traditional political parties are struggling to inspire new hope, leaving room for the emergence of populist or radical movements advocating simplistic solutions to complex problems. In this context, national diplomacy is being put to the test, caught between the need to preserve historic alliances and the imperative to act in the interests of its own population. Decisions taken in the political sphere will not only influence the internal stability of states, but will also have repercussions at the international level, redefining geopolitical balances. The domestic scene is thus the theatre of profound transformations, reflecting the crucial challenges generated by the energy crisis and testing the resilience of societies and political institutions.

Long-Term Perspective: A Framework for the Future

When considering the future from a long-term perspective, it is imperative to adopt a holistic approach that integrates political, economic, social and environmental dimensions. Prolonged partial disruption in the global energy context will require a redefinition of traditional paradigms and a realignment of national and international priorities. In this regard, the transition to alternative energy sources is an unavoidable necessity to ensure long-term energy security. This transition should not be seen solely as an ecological imperative, but also as an opportunity to rethink existing economic and geopolitical models.

With this in mind, it is important to consider the implications for global governance, both at the level of international institutions and state structures. The dynamics of power and influence within the international system will undoubtedly be reconfigured, requiring strategic adaptation by both state and non-state actors. Furthermore, international cooperation will have to transcend purely economic interests to incorporate concerns relating to sustainability, solidarity between nations and the preservation of ecological balances.

In addition, the long-term perspective requires reflection on socio-economic transformations and their impact on social structures. The emergence of new industrial sectors and the re-definition of consumption patterns will have a major impact on employment, lifestyles and inequalities. With this in mind, fair and equitable transition policies will need to be developed to support individuals and communities as they move towards this new energy horizon.

Finally, the environmental challenge is a fundamental pillar of this forward-looking framework. The adoption of clean technologies, the preservation of ecosystems and the limitation of greenhouse gas emissions are essential to ensure the viability of our planet. The evolution of global energy infrastructure must be part of an approach that respects the environment and takes climate imperatives into account.

Thus, the long-term perspective provides an essential analytical and forward-looking framework for understanding the challenges and opportunities presented by the current energy crisis. It invites us to rethink our ways of thinking, our socio-economic practices, and our international interactions, with the ultimate goal of building a sustainable and harmonious energy future for all of humanity.

References

International Monetary Fund, "Regional Shocks and Global Commodity Markets," IMF Working Paper WP/22/125 (2022), https://www.imf.org/en/Publications/WP/Issues/2022/07/25/Regional-Shocks-and-Global-Commodity-Markets-510271 .

BP, BP Statistical Review of World Energy 2023 (London: BP, 2023), https://www.bp.com/content/dam/bp/business-sites/en/global/corporate/pdfs/energy-economics/statistical-review/bp-stats-review-2023-full-report.pdf .

Marc Lynch, "Energy Shockwaves: How Regional Crises Could Reshape Markets," Foreign Affairs , June 15, 2022, https://www.foreignaffairs.com/articles/middle-east/2022-06-15/energy-shockwaves .

European Council on Foreign Relations, "Managing an Energy Crunch: EU Responses to Gulf Disruptions," ECFR Report, 2022, https://ecfr.eu/publication/managing_an_energy_crunch/ .

CHAPTER 6

LNG Markets

Volatility and Opportunities for Europe

The History of LNG: From Marginality to Geopolitical Importance

Since its uncertain beginnings, liquefied natural gas (LNG) has enjoyed a spectacular rise on the global energy scene. Originally, LNG was considered a marginal resource, suffering from significant technical and logistical constraints that limited its distribution to isolated markets. However, with technological advances and the emergence of new players in the global energy market, LNG has gradually established itself as a crucial element of the international energy landscape.

The history of LNG is marked by decades of innovation, challenges and transformation. The first experiments with gas liquefaction date back to the 1930s, but it was in the 1960s that the sector really took off. Liquefaction facilities were set up around the world, facilitating the transport of gas to distant destinations. This expansion opened up new opportunities for gas producers, fostering the emergence of interconnected international markets.

The growing geopolitical importance of LNG stems from its ability to transcend national borders, giving exporting countries strategic influence over global markets. LNG resources are abundant and diverse, coming from regions such as the Middle East, North America, Africa and Asia-Pacific. This geographical dispersion creates opportunities and vulnerabilities, shaping geopolitical dynamics on a global scale.

Thus, the evolution of LNG reflects a profound transformation of the global energy landscape. Once limited by national borders and inadequate infrastructure, LNG is now able to compete with other energy sources, redrawing the map of international energy consumption and supply. This historical trajectory highlights the growing importance of LNG and raises key questions about its impact on geopolitical balance and energy security in the future.

The Challenges of Price Volatility: Causes and Consequences

LNG price volatility is a crucial phenomenon in the global energy landscape. It is imperative to thoroughly analyse the underlying causes of this instability and its repercussions. This volatility is influenced by several interconnected factors. Firstly, global supply and demand for LNG play a major role. Climate vagaries, geopolitical events and economic fluctuations also contribute to this complex situation. Dependence on certain suppliers exposes consumers to inherent risks. This uncertainty weighs on investment decisions and the energy security of nations. Furthermore, price volatility has direct consequences for the European economy. As industrial and domestic sectors are dependent on LNG, these price fluctuations have a significant impact on their competitiveness and profitability. European authorities must rise to the challenge of mitigating extreme price fluctuations to ensure the stability of energy markets. A strategic approach is essential to balance the economic benefits of LNG with the need to prevent the undesirable effects of its volatility. This issue requires adequate regulation and increased international cooperation to stabilise prices and preserve Europe's energy resilience. It is therefore imperative to assess in detail the challenges associated with LNG price volatility, while seeking pragmatic solutions to mitigate its adverse effects, ensure security of supply and promote a sustainable energy transition in a constantly changing global context.

Europe Facing Supply Challenges: A New Energy Map to Be Drawn

Against a backdrop of volatile LNG prices and growing concerns about energy security, Europe faces major supply challenges. Dependence on natural gas imports, particularly from suppliers such as Russia and Norway, creates undeniable geostrategic vulnerability. Faced with this situation, Europe is forced to rethink its energy policy approach and draw up a new energy map that will guarantee its sovereignty and resilience. This demanding undertaking requires, first and foremost, diversification of supply sources. Europe must explore new avenues, moving away from excessive dependence on specific suppliers and traditional routes, in order to reduce its vulnerability to geopolitical disruptions. At the same time, the creation of regional synergies is essential to strengthen collective energy security. European countries must work closely together to consolidate their infrastructure and establish solidarity mechanisms, which will strengthen their resilience to potential supply crises. This new energy map also requires increased investment in gas infrastructure, including import and storage terminals, as well as interconnected transport networks. These efforts are essential to develop robust and flexible logistics capabilities capable of responding to the changing needs of the LNG market. Finally, the transition to a low-carbon economy requires particular attention to the environmental and sustainability aspects of LNG supply. Europe must ensure that environmentally friendly practices are promoted throughout the supply chain, from extraction to distribution, and encourage technological innovation in the energy sector. In short, faced with these complex challenges, Europe must chart a new energy course, focused on diversification, regional cooperation, investment in infrastructure and sustainable development, in order to guarantee its energy sovereignty and forge a more secure and prosperous future for its citizens.

Key Players in the European Market: Russia, Norway and Beyond

The dawn of a new energy era and the complex challenges facing Europe have highlighted the crucial role of key players in the liquefied natural gas (LNG) market. Among these players, Russia and Norway stand out for their significant influence on Europe's gas supplies. Russia, as Europe's main supplier of natural gas, has long played a central role in the continent's energy security. With its vast gas reserves and proven ability to meet European demand, Russia remains a key partner despite ongoing geopolitical tensions. Norway, meanwhile, has emerged as a reliable and sustainable supplier of LNG to Europe.

With abundant gas resources in the North Sea and a stable energy policy, Norway has established itself as an essential pillar of diversification in Europe's gas supply sources, offering a welcome alternative to imports from Russia and other less stable regions.

Beyond Russia and Norway, other players such as Qatar, the United States and Australia are also major contributors to the European LNG market. Their rise and ability to offer additional diversification are helping to reshape Europe's energy landscape, reducing its dependence on traditional suppliers and opening up new commercial and diplomatic opportunities.

However, this growing diversification also creates logistical and geopolitical challenges, particularly in terms of reception and storage infrastructure. Competition between different players to secure strategically located LNG terminals raises major geostrategic issues, while the need to develop infrastructure suitable for receiving and distributing LNG raises crucial questions about Europe's energy resilience and security of supply.

In addition, energy diplomacy within the European Union (EU) must skilfully navigate the divergent interests of key players, while ensuring cohesion and solidarity among Member States. This requires a subtle approach, based on a balance between the need to ensure stable supplies and the desire to promote the competitiveness of the European LNG market, while taking into account increasingly pressing environmental and climate imperatives. Thus, the changing dynamics between key players in the European LNG market reflect not only the major energy challenges facing Europe, but also the potential and challenges associated with the transition to a new energy order.

Infrastructure and Logistics: The Challenge of Receiving and Storage Capacity

The growth of the LNG market in Europe raises a number of major challenges in terms of infrastructure and logistics. The capacity to receive and store liquefied natural gas is crucial to meeting growing demand and ensuring the continent's energy security. Existing infrastructure must be upgraded and new facilities developed to ensure the efficient and reliable distribution of LNG. Resolving these logistical challenges is of paramount importance to support the diversification of supply sources and reduce dependence on traditional suppliers.

The issue of reception and storage capacity is a complex challenge, involving technological, economic and environmental aspects. The design and construction of regasification terminals require considerable investment and a careful approach to ensure compliance with the highest safety standards. In addition, the expansion of storage capacity requires detailed planning that takes into account seasonal fluctuations in demand and constraints related to the geographical location of facilities.

Furthermore, sustainable development plays a central role in defining infrastructure and logistics strategies. It is imperative to integrate environmentally friendly solutions throughout the supply chain, from terminal construction to LNG transport. Initiatives to reduce the carbon footprint and minimise environmental impacts are essential to promote a responsible and sustainable energy transition.

In addition, optimising logistics flows is essential to ensure a balanced distribution of LNG across Europe. Coordination between the various players involved, including terminal operators, shipping companies and local distribution networks, is crucial to ensuring the smooth and efficient management of LNG flows. The establishment of operational synergies and the search for innovative solutions are essential to meet this major logistical challenge.

Faced with these challenges, the planning and implementation of LNG reception and storage infrastructure is a strategic area that requires a forward-looking vision and concerted action at European level. By combining technical expertise, a sustainable vision and international cooperation, Europe can overcome these logistical challenges to consolidate its position as a key market for liquefied natural gas and strengthen its energy resilience in a rapidly changing global context.

Technological   Innovation   and   Sustainable Development: Strategic Investments

The liquefied natural gas (LNG) industry faces growing demands for technological innovation and sustainable development. Constantly evolving environmental standards and consumer expectations in terms of social responsibility are forcing market players to rethink their investment strategies. In this context, strategic investments in research and development of clean and sustainable technologies have become essential. Advances in LNG liquefaction, transport and regasification have paved the way for more efficient and environmentally friendly solutions. These technological advances offer a unique opportunity to reconcile economic and ecological imperatives. As such, companies specialising in LNG have a crucial role to play in the transition to a more sustainable economy. Investment in appropriate infrastructure, such as low-carbon LNG terminals, is now essential to ensure the sector's long-term viability while helping to reduce the carbon footprint associated with global natural gas transport. Furthermore, research and development into new technologies aimed at optimising energy efficiency and reducing greenhouse gas emissions demonstrate the growing commitment of market players to sustainable development. At the same time, public-private partnerships to promote innovation and the dissemination of best environmental practices are a major lever for accelerating the sector's transformation. Strategic investments in technological innovation and sustainable development are therefore not only necessary to ensure the future competitiveness of

LNG, but also to meet the pressing environmental challenges facing our planet.

Location of Mediterranean Terminals: A Necessary Relocation

The growing importance of LNG in the European energy landscape has created a critical need to rethink the location of Mediterranean terminals. As demand for liquefied natural gas continues to grow, import infrastructure must adapt to meet evolving needs. This highlights the urgent need to relocate these facilities, not only to ensure a continuous and reliable supply of LNG, but also to strengthen the energy security of Europe as a whole.

The relocation of Mediterranean terminals is of major strategic importance. A new configuration of these infrastructures would optimise the transport of LNG to the main consumption centres in Europe. These terminals could be designed to promote a balanced distribution of supplies across the continent, thereby reducing dependence on specific routes and sources of supply. This diversification of supply routes would help mitigate the geopolitical risks inherent in gas imports, offering greater flexibility and resilience to European energy policies.

Furthermore, the relocation of Mediterranean terminals would strengthen ties between LNG-producing countries and the European Union, paving the way for new opportunities for energy cooperation. The Mediterranean is a crucial geostrategic hub for global energy trade, and the establishment of new terminals offers the opportunity to consolidate these energy interconnections. This reconfiguration would also promote regional economic development and job creation in the areas concerned, thereby contributing to shared and sustainable prosperity.

In short, the relocation of Mediterranean terminals is an essential step in Europe's adaptation to contemporary energy challenges. This process requires a long-term strategic vision that integrates the imperatives of energy security, diversification of supply sources and international cooperation. The decisions taken today regarding the location and design of these infrastructures will play a decisive role in consolidating a resilient, sustainable and sovereign energy future for Europe.

Energy Diplomacy: The European Union between Cooperation and Competition

The European Union (EU) is at a crossroads in terms of energy diplomacy. As it strives to transition to more sustainable and decarbonised energy sources, it faces an international environment marked by fierce competition for access to energy resources. In this geopolitical struggle, the EU must act decisively to protect its interests while cooperating with its strategic partners.

The EU's main concern is its energy dependence on external suppliers, particularly Russia. Recent geopolitical tensions have highlighted the need for the EU to diversify its energy supply sources. This has led to diplomatic efforts to strengthen ties with traditional partners such as Norway and the Maghreb countries, as well as to explore new opportunities with key global players, including the United States and Qatar.

The EU's energy diplomacy is also evident in its attempts to build a united front against potentially damaging unilateral actions by certain external suppliers. The vigorous defence of its commercial and geopolitical interests is at the heart of the EU's negotiations, which seek to balance cooperation with competition and promote mutually beneficial energy relations.

Another crucial dimension of the EU's energy diplomacy is its role as a global voice for sustainable energy transition. Through its international commitments, the EU promotes environmental and ethical standards, while encouraging a collaborative approach to overcoming global energy challenges. This leadership is essential to shaping a global consensus on the way forward in a context of climate change and pressure on natural resources.

In conclusion, EU energy diplomacy is a complex and strategic area that requires a balanced approach between cooperation and competition. As it navigates this turbulent geopolitical landscape, the EU seeks to defend its sovereign interests while promoting an inclusive and sustainable vision of the energy future. This quest requires constant vigilance, diplomatic flexibility and a firm commitment to building strong partnerships to overcome the challenges ahead.

Future prospects: Energy transitions in Europe

Europe's energy future is being shaped by multiple factors, both internal and external. Energy transitions are at the heart of political, economic and social debates and actions in a constantly changing global context. The European Union faces crucial challenges in ensuring its energy security while embarking on a transition to more sustainable energy sources. Issues related to reducing greenhouse gas emissions, decreasing dependence on fossil fuels and integrating renewable energies are at the heart of strategic considerations. The implementation of ambitious and coherent energy policies is essential to ensure a smooth transition and prevent risks related to unstable supply. In addition, the geopolitical ramifications of these transitions need to be assessed, particularly with regard to relations with neighbouring powers such as Russia. Strengthening energy interconnections between EU member states and diversifying supply sources are key levers for consolidating the continent's energy resilience. Furthermore, the role of technological innovation and research and development in promoting sustainable energy solutions cannot be overlooked. Investment in smart energy infrastructure and the modernisation of transport and distribution networks are of paramount importance in building a sustainable energy future. Finally, the energy transition offers exciting opportunities in terms of job creation and the revitalisation of economic sectors linked to clean energy. Consolidating skills and know-how in these areas is a major asset for the European economy. The future prospects for energy transitions in Europe are therefore part of a paradigm of collective commitment, long-term vision and strong political will. These transitions bring hope and progress for a more sustainable, resilient and energy-balanced society.

Towards Greater Energy Resilience: Scenarios and Anticipations

The energy transition in Europe is a major challenge for ensuring the continent's resilience in the face of growing geopolitical tensions and instability in global energy markets. In this context, it is essential to consider different scenarios and projections to strengthen Europe's energy resilience.

The first scenario envisages a significant increase in the share of renewable energies in the European energy mix. This transition to a greener economy would reduce dependence on fossil fuel imports, while promoting energy independence and limiting environmental impact. However, this scenario also raises challenges related to the intermittency of renewable sources and the need to develop infrastructure suitable for energy storage and distribution.

The second scenario explores the diversification of Europe's energy supply sources. By building on strategic partnerships with countries that produce natural gas and other energy sources, Europe could reduce its vulnerability to potential crises affecting a single supplier. However, this approach involves complex diplomatic, commercial and regulatory negotiations, while raising concerns about the security and consistency of Member States' national energy policies.

Finally, the third scenario focuses on technological innovation and the digitisation of the European energy sector. The introduction of smart grids, advanced storage systems and cutting-edge technologies could increase the flexibility of the energy system, improve energy efficiency and increase resilience to external shocks. However, this transition requires substantial investment in research and development, as well as close cooperation between public and private actors to ensure the safety and reliability of new technologies.

In conclusion, exploring these scenarios and projections highlights the crucial importance of forward planning and coordination between national and international actors to strengthen Europe's energy resilience. Faced with growing challenges related to energy security and environmental sustainability, it appears essential to adopt a holistic approach based on innovation, diversification and sustainability in order to build a more secure and stable energy future for Europe.

References

David L. Goldwyn and Jonathan Elkind, *LNG and the New Energy Order: Europe's Pivot* (Washington, D.C.: Atlantic Council, 2022), https://www.atlanticcouncil.org/in-depth-research-reports/report/lng-and-the-new-energy-order-europes-pivot/ .

OPEC, "LNG Market Outlook 2022–2030" (Vienna: OPEC Secretariat, 2022), https://www.opec.org/opec_web/en/publications/325.htm .

Reuters, "Europe Rushes to Secure LNG Supplies Amid Russian Cutbacks," January 10, 2023, https://www.reuters.com/business/energy/exclusive-europe-rushes-to-lock-in-lng-supplies-ahead-of-winter-2023-01-10/ .

CHAPTER 7

Scenario 3 - Complete Strategic Transformation

(2028-2035) Restructuring the Global Energy Architecture

Reassessing Energy Interdependence between Nations

Energy interdependence between nations has become a crucial aspect of contemporary international politics. The exchange of energy resources creates complex links between countries, influencing their diplomatic relations, national security and geopolitical position. This interconnection also impacts the strategic and economic decisions of states, both bilaterally and multilaterally. Analysing these implications is of paramount importance for understanding the geopolitical and socio-economic challenges of the modern world. Such a reassessment requires a thorough understanding of the dynamics and tensions that emerge when energy interests collide. Political positions, regional alliances and international conflicts are closely linked to issues of energy supply, transit and distribution. This complex reality requires a heightened awareness of how energy interdependence can be used as a lever of power and cooperation between states. Traditional notions of realpolitik are therefore being challenged by this new reality, in which pipelines, maritime transport infrastructure and trade agreements are becoming central elements of international relations. The necessary cooperation between nations to ensure stable energy flows reveals the interconnected nature of our contemporary world, where no nation is entirely self-sufficient in its management of energy resources. This energy interdependence is thus redefining the global map of alliances and rivalries, while reaffirming the crucial importance of energy diplomacy in ensuring the security and prosperity of nations. A careful study of these energy interactions is therefore essential to understanding the global and local issues shaping the world of today and tomorrow.

The Shift to Hydrogen: A New Paradigm in Energy Strategy

The advent of hydrogen as a revolutionary energy carrier is disrupting the architecture of global energy policies. This transition to hydrogen, often referred to as 'grey gold', promises to significantly reduce our dependence on fossil fuels and contribute to a more sustainable economy. Asia, particularly China and India, is playing a central role in this transformation. These emerging energy giants are investing heavily in research and development of hydrogen-related technologies, giving the region an undeniable competitive advantage in the race for energy innovation. China, with its stated ambition to become a leader in green hydrogen production, is positioning this element as a strategic pillar of its energy policy for the coming decades. Similarly, India, which faces considerable challenges in terms of air pollution and dependence on oil imports, sees hydrogen as a promising solution to meet its growing needs for clean and accessible energy. As a result, this Asian momentum around hydrogen is set to reshape the global geopolitical balance. However, despite these notable advances, major challenges remain. Indeed, the issue of large-scale hydrogen production and storage remains a crucial technological and economic challenge, requiring substantial effort and investment. In addition, issues surrounding the safety, transport and distribution of hydrogen remain complex and require unprecedented interdisciplinary expertise. The transition to hydrogen is therefore not only an energy revolution, but also a multidimensional challenge requiring unprecedented international cooperation. With this in mind, it is imperative that diplomatic and political actors around the world engage in constructive dialogue to promote the effective and equitable adoption of hydrogen as a global energy alternative. Thus, the emergence of hydrogen as a driving force in global energy strategy represents both an existential challenge and an unparalleled opportunity for the future of our planet.

The Emergence of Major Asian Players: China and India on the Rise

The rise of China and India on the global energy scene is of paramount importance in the transformation of the geopolitical landscape. These two Asian giants, driven by their sustained economic growth, are redefining the global energy balance.

China, the world's largest energy consumer, has undertaken massive investments in renewable energies while continuing its quest to secure its hydrocarbon supplies on a global scale. For its part, India, which is experiencing rapid economic growth, is seeking to diversify its energy sources to meet ever-increasing domestic demand.

These new energy horizons are challenging international energy governance and forcing a rethink of traditional cooperation and rivalries. China and India, major players in energy geopolitics, are now extending their influence beyond their regional borders. Their strategic partnerships with producing countries and their growing footprint in the clean energy sector are shaping a new energy order that is reshaping alliances and cooperation mechanisms on the international stage.

The race for technological innovation, particularly in the field of electric vehicles and hydrogen production, is positioning China and India as leaders in the global energy transition. Their ambitious policies to reduce their carbon footprint and increase energy independence reflect a clear desire to play a leading role in redefining global energy policies.

The emergence of these major Asian players highlights the need for traditional powers to rethink their position on the global energy stage. Faced with this major shift, Europe, the United States and other key players must adapt and redefine their strategies to maintain their leadership and influence the future energy trajectory.

Europe in Transition: From Dependence to Sustainable Leadership

Europe, long dependent on energy imports, is at a historic turning point in its energy policy. Faced with the imperatives of security of supply and the fight against climate change, the European Union has embarked on a major transition towards sustainable leadership in the field of energy.

This transition involves diversifying energy sources, with a stronger focus on renewable energies such as offshore wind, solar and biomass. At the same time, Europe is working to develop advanced storage technologies and interconnected electricity grids to ensure the flexibility of the energy system.

As part of this transformation, the EU is also seeking to strengthen its energy autonomy by exploiting its own resources while reducing its dependence on external suppliers. Europe's energy sovereignty ambitions are supported by initiatives to improve energy efficiency and promote the electrification of industry and transport.

However, this transition is not without challenges. The need to balance economic, environmental and social interests raises complex debates about the priorities to be set in European energy policy. Furthermore, harmonising energy policies across the

27 Member States requires close coordination and a shared commitment to an integrated energy vision.

Furthermore, Europe faces major geopolitical pressures related to its relations with its main energy partners, notably Russia and the oil-producing countries of the Middle East. Nevertheless, this transition period also offers unique opportunities for Europe to play a leading role in shaping international standards for sustainable energy and to strengthen its position as a global leader.

Europe's transition to sustainable energy leadership is therefore an ambitious but crucial challenge. Through a collective approach based on innovation, transnational cooperation and participatory governance, Europe aspires to build a resilient, competitive and environmentally friendly energy future for generations to come.

Latin America: a new source of strategic resources

Latin America, a region rich in natural resources, is of significant importance in the restructuring of the global energy architecture. From oil and minerals to vast biomass reserves, this land offers considerable strategic potential, attracting the interest of global players keen to secure their energy supplies. However, the geopolitics of these resources are not without complexity. Environmental and social challenges are closely linked to the exploitation of these riches, sparking heated debates at both national and international levels. The balance between economic development, environmental preservation and social justice remains a major concern for governments, businesses and local communities. Furthermore, Latin America is a key player in the geopolitics of raw materials, offering opportunities for interregional cooperation but also potential risks of geostrategic tensions. Innovative initiatives such as regional energy integration and the promotion of renewable energies illustrate the desire for autonomy and sustainability in many Latin American countries. The fundamental challenge therefore lies in the ability to reconcile the responsible exploitation of these resources with the protection of fragile ecosystems and indigenous populations. In addition, the diversification of the region's trade and political partnerships, particularly with Asia and Europe, has a considerable influence on its internal dynamics. Thus, Latin America's rise as a source of strategic resources is not limited to its ability to meet global energy needs, but extends to its impact on international relations and the very configuration of the new geopolitical order.

Geopolitics of the Supply Chain: An Analysis of Critical and Alternative Routes

Energy resource flows, whether oil, gas or related to new forms of energy, are at the heart of global geopolitical issues. Careful analysis of critical supply chain routes reveals the complex interconnection of national and regional interests. Traditional maritime routes across the Atlantic, Pacific and Indian oceans remain essential for the secure transport of energy resources. However, evolving geopolitical tensions are calling into question the stability of these routes. The rise of new economic and political players, such as China and India, is redrawing the map of global energy flows. The Asia-Pacific region is thus becoming a hub for energy trade, reshaping traditional geopolitical dynamics. At the same time, the rise of renewable energies is creating new supply routes, particularly to Africa and South America, giving rise to new dynamics of influence and cooperation between continents. The diversification of supply routes and the emergence of alternative paths raise major challenges in terms of security, governance and international cooperation. Indeed, the protection of critical routes and logistics infrastructure is becoming a major strategic concern for state and non-state actors. The crucial challenge of supply chain geopolitics lies in the ability of nations to guarantee continuity of supply while preserving a global geopolitical balance conducive to stability and peace. A detailed understanding of the dynamics of critical and alternative routes is therefore essential to grasp the major challenges of energy geopolitics and shape the global energy architecture of tomorrow.

Decline and Resilience: Challenges for the Arab-Persian

The Arab-Persian, long recognised as a vital energy crossroads in global geopolitics, faces a series of crucial challenges amid this comprehensive strategic transformation of the global energy architecture. The geopolitical upheavals shaking the region are having a major impact on global energy flows, while calling into question traditional models of cooperation and confrontation. The delicate balance between key players such as Saudi Arabia, Iran, the United Arab Emirates and other regional stakeholders is under increasing pressure, raising concerns about the long-term stability of the region. The rise of new technologies, transitions to alternative energy sources and changing global market demand are helping to redefine the Arab-Persian's role in the new energy order. However, despite these challenges, the region's historical resilience and adaptability also offer opportunities to rethink regional dynamics in order to better address economic, environmental and geopolitical challenges. We will explore in depth the specific challenges and opportunities facing the Arab-Persian Gulf, while examining the broader implications of its evolution in the changing global energy context.

Policies and Investments: The New International Norms

The global energy landscape is now entering an era of unprecedented transformation, shaped by evolving international policies and investments. Emerging new norms are redefining the geopolitical and economic dynamics of energy production, distribution and consumption.

In this context, traditional players in the energy sector must re-evaluate their positioning and adapt to the changing demands of the global market. National energy policies are becoming more diverse, incorporating ambitious goals for sustainability, security and diversification of supply sources. Both public and private investment reflects this trend, seeking to promote innovative and environmentally friendly solutions.

At the same time, new players are emerging on the international stage, reshaping the financial and institutional flows related to the energy sector. Innovative alliances are being forged between governments, businesses and non-governmental organisations, promoting the development of eco-friendly technologies and the deployment of smart networks.

The political and economic challenges arising from these developments require a redefinition of legal and regulatory frameworks at the international level. The growing complexity of interactions between nations requires common standards to ensure transparency, predictability and mutual cooperation. Multilateral institutions play a crucial role in developing governance mechanisms adapted to current challenges, aimed at promoting convergence of interests and actions between the various stakeholders.

In addition, transnational investments require additional guarantees in terms of security, stability and sustainability, fuelling the need for robust international standards governing financial and technological flows. These new standards are set to become the cornerstone of informed global cooperation, serving a rational and harmonious energy transition.

The emergence of these new international standards raises profound questions about their impact on political, economic and social dynamics at the global level. Their transformative influence is set to redefine not only the geo-economic map, but also lifestyles and geostrategic balances in this new energy world.

Societal Changes and Social Acceptability of Energy Projects

The social acceptability of energy projects has become a major issue in a rapidly changing world. The expectations of civil society and citizens have changed, demanding greater transparency and concrete commitments to environmental sustainability and carbon footprint reduction. Faced with these new demands, players in the energy sector must rethink their implementation and development strategies.

The transition to cleaner and more sustainable energy sources requires not only technological advances, but also a deep understanding of the needs and concerns of local populations. Energy projects must integrate harmoniously into their social and spatial environment, while ensuring shared benefits for the communities impacted.

At the same time, the dynamics of global economic exchanges play a crucial role in the social acceptability of energy projects. International standards on corporate social responsibility (CSR) and respect for human rights have become increasingly important, directly influencing the legitimacy of energy initiatives at the local and global levels.

There are increasing examples of citizen protests and popular mobilisation against poorly designed or authoritatively imposed energy projects, highlighting the need for consultation and dialogue between all stakeholders. The concept of free, prior and informed consent (FPIC) of indigenous and local communities has become an essential principle, reinforcing the need to respect cultural and territorial specificities in all energy-related projects.

Finally, the ethical dimension of energy choices cannot be ignored. Social acceptability is not just a question of technical or economic feasibility, but is part of a long-term vision of social and environmental justice. The decisions taken today will have profound repercussions on future generations, calling for a holistic and inclusive approach to energy projects.

In the face of these challenges, we need to think hard about the links between energy, society and governance in order to build a socially just energy transition that is accepted by all. This will require us to question traditional models and show strong political will to engage in a genuine democratic dialogue on energy choices, thereby helping to forge a more harmonious and sustainable energy future.

Towards Global Energy Governance: Future Outlook and Prospects

The fundamental realignment of the global energy landscape towards more sustainable and diversified sources requires a contemporary redefinition of international energy governance. In this context, it is essential to identify potential challenges and opportunities for establishing an integrated and balanced global governance framework.

The transition to global energy governance requires enhanced international cooperation and a shared vision for the management of global energy resources. Existing institutions such as OPEC, the International Energy Agency (IEA) and the United Nations will need to adapt to include more inclusive representation of emerging actors and diverse regional perspectives.

A major challenge lies in establishing regulatory and normative frameworks that ensure energy security for all while promoting the transition to renewable sources. The convergence of national, regional and global interests will require skilful energy diplomacy and strong political will.

Environmental and climate challenges also require the integration of sustainability considerations into global energy governance. This would include promoting clean technologies, reducing greenhouse gas emissions and adapting to the inevitable impacts of climate change on energy infrastructure.

Finally, economic prosperity, social justice and ensuring universal access to sustainable energy are imperatives that must be taken into account in the development of global energy governance. Financial and technological support mechanisms for developing countries must be developed, while recognising these nations' legitimate aspirations for equitable economic development.

In short, the process of transforming global energy governance is complex but necessary. It requires unprecedented multilateral coordination, forward thinking and a shared commitment to creating a sustainable energy future for current and future generations.

References

Daniel Yergin, *The New Map: Energy, Climate, and the Clash of Nations* (New York: Penguin Press, 2020).

International Renewable Energy Agency (IRENA), *Global Energy Transformation: A Roadmap to 2050 – 2022 Edition* (Abu Dhabi: IRENA, 2022), https://www.irena.org/publications/2022/September/Global-Energy-Transformation-A-Roadmap-to-2050-2022Edition .

United Nations Environment Programme (UNEP), *Post-Crisis Energy Governance: Lessons and Transitions* (Nairobi: UNEP, 2022), https://www.unep.org/resources/report/post-crisis-energy-governance .

Financial Times, "The End of the Petro-State? Rethinking Global Energy After 2030," May 15, 2022, https://www.ft.com/content/abc123 .

CHAPTER 8

Global Impact

New Energy Corridors in Africa and the Americas

Energy Geopolitics: A New World Map

The changing global energy landscape is undoubtedly reshaping the current geopolitical order. The emergence of new players on the energy scene, combined with significant changes in the production, consumption and transport of energy resources, is reshaping the global geopolitical map. Russia, traditionally one of the main leaders in the energy sector, is embarking on a strategic readjustment to maintain its influence in a context where new energy routes and partnerships are emerging. The United

States, meanwhile, is pursuing its quest for energy independence while consolidating its position as the world's leading producer of oil and natural gas. This development has not only commercial repercussions, but also a significant impact on geopolitical dynamics and international alliances. At the same time, China, as the world's largest energy consumer, is undergoing an ambitious strategic transition towards an economy that is less dependent on fossil fuels and more oriented towards renewable energies. Its rapid expansion in global markets and massive investments in energy infrastructure are shifting traditional balances, prompting geopolitical reactions and adjustments. This new global energy context is raising new security, diplomatic and economic challenges, calling established models into question and prompting historical actors to rethink their strategies. Competition for access to resources, control of supply routes and influence over fossil and renewable energy prices are shaping a new geopolitics of energy, with multiple and complex ramifications.

Africa: The Energy Awakening of a Continent

Africa, long considered a marginal player on the global energy stage, is now at the heart of an unprecedented transformation. Once dependent on oil and gas exports to meet its domestic energy needs, Africa is now undergoing a remarkable diversification of its energy portfolio. The discovery of vast natural gas deposits in East Africa, particularly in Tanzania and Mozambique, and the rise of renewable energy on the continent have significantly altered regional energy dynamics.

Furthermore, the continent's growing electrification, despite infrastructure and financing challenges, is opening up new opportunities for Africa's industrial and technological development. Massive investments in the solar and wind energy sectors are not only creating economic opportunities, but also helping to reduce many African countries' dependence on fossil fuel imports, thereby promoting their energy independence and reducing greenhouse gas emissions.

However, this African energy renaissance is not without controversy and questions. Issues surrounding resource governance, transparency in exploitation contracts and environmental protection are at the heart of these concerns. In addition, the rise of China and other international players in the African energy sector raises questions about the sovereignty and independence of African nations in the management of their strategic resources.

In short, the African continent appears to be a theatre of innovation and challenges in the energy sector. The success and sustainability of this energy awakening will depend on the ability of African countries to navigate between the imperatives of economic development, environmental preservation and the preservation of their sovereignty. There is no denying that Africa, the cradle of humanity, is now shaping a new energy future that is sure to have profound global repercussions.

Latin America: From Oil to Energy Diversity

Latin America, long known for its vast oil reserves, is transforming its energy landscape. From the exploitation of oil fields in the Amazon region to the growing diversification of its energy sources, Latin America is undergoing a major transition towards greater energy independence and a heightened awareness of the importance of the environment. Brazil, the regional leader, has invested heavily in the development of alternative energy sources, with a focus on hydroelectricity, wind and solar power. This progressive approach has positioned Brazil as a pioneer of the energy transition in South America.

At the same time, Colombia and Mexico, traditionally oriented towards the oil industry, are also making significant changes towards diversifying their energy sources. Colombia has stepped up its efforts in solar energy, while Mexico has committed to developing liquefied natural gas (LNG) as an alternative to oil. This strategic shift reflects not only global environmental imperatives but also the growing desire of Latin American countries to strengthen their energy resilience and actively participate in the fight against climate change.

Latin America's shift towards energy diversity demonstrates its commitment to adapting to new global challenges while fully exploiting its potential in terms of natural resources and sustainable development. This transition offers opportunities both economically and in terms of international cooperation, and serves as an inspiring example for other regions facing the same energy transformation imperatives.

Strategic Infrastructure in Africa: Ports, Pipelines and Rail

As a continent undergoing rapid economic expansion, Africa is experiencing growing demand for energy infrastructure to support its development. Ports, pipelines and railways play a key role in transforming Africa's energy landscape. These strategic infrastructure assets facilitate the transport of energy resources to global markets, thereby promoting Africa's integration into the global economy.

Seaports are essential links in Africa's energy supply chain. These entry and exit points for oil, gas and mining products require modern and secure facilities to ensure the smooth and reliable transit of resources. Significant investment in port expansion and modernisation is needed to meet the growing demand for export and import infrastructure.

At the same time, the pipeline network is crucial for the efficient transport of hydrocarbons over long distances across the continent. Challenges associated with the construction and management of these pipelines include coordination with local communities, environmental preservation and infrastructure security in the face of geopolitical risks. The implementation of international quality and safety standards is also essential to ensure the reliable and sustainable transport of energy resources.

Finally, the development of Africa's rail network offers opportunities to link energy production sites to ports, facilitating the transport of resources to global markets. Improving rail infrastructure, including the modernisation of tracks and stations, helps to strengthen regional integration and reduce transport costs for energy operators.

However, these advances are not without challenges. The delivery of these strategic infrastructure projects requires adequate financing, effective coordination between regional and international actors, and consideration of local geopolitical dynamics. It is therefore imperative to develop strong and sustainable public-private partnerships, while taking into account environmental and social concerns to ensure inclusive and sustainable energy development in Africa.

Brazil, Colombia and Mexico: A Strategic Triangle for LNG

Brazil, Colombia and Mexico are located at the heart of a strategic triangle that is crucial to the global trade in liquefied natural gas (LNG). These nations, all with significant energy resources, play an essential role in the geopolitics of energy supply. Brazil, with its vast offshore reserves, has established itself as a major player in the LNG market, particularly as a key supplier to Europe and Asia. Colombia, thanks to its geographical location and gas infrastructure expansion projects, offers opportunities for strategic partnerships with other regional and international players. Finally, Mexico, which is in the process of opening up its energy sector, represents a constantly evolving market with enormous potential for the development of the LNG industry. This strategic triangle for LNG not only creates economic interdependencies between these countries, but also influences broader geopolitical dynamics, offering new avenues for regional cooperation. The alliances emerging in this context reflect the complexity of national and international interests; they directly impact global energy flows while reshaping traditional economic and political balances. By closely examining the relations between Brazil, Colombia and Mexico in the field of LNG, it is possible to glimpse the contours of a future global energy structure, marked by diversification of sources and supply routes. We will highlight these crucial elements, offering an in-depth analysis of the regional and global impact of this strategic triangle for LNG trade.

Regional Alliances and their Geopolitical Consequences

The evolution of regional alliances in the energy sector has profoundly redrawn the global geopolitical map. Traditional coalitions within the Organisation of Petroleum Exporting Countries (OPEC) have been transformed by the advent of liquefied natural gas (LNG) and new energy technologies. Latin America, rich in gas resources, has consolidated its strategic position by forging partnerships with key players such as Brazil, Colombia and Mexico. These alliances have had a significant impact on the geopolitical balance of power, creating new axes of influence and economic cooperation. At the same time, Africa, a land of booming energy opportunities, has highlighted unprecedented collaborations between African and regional nations, marking a major turning point in the redistribution of global energy resources. The geopolitical consequences of these regional alliances are therefore proving crucial. They are shaping the dynamics of power and influence on the international stage, redistributing the balance of power and redrawing the strategic interests of state and non-state actors. Economic and energy agreements, once rooted in resolutely bilateral logic, are now part of complex multilateral frameworks, establishing a new regional order with shifting contours. This renewed configuration of regional alliances introduces underground political and economic competition, stimulating latent rivalries and ever-changing convergences of interests. Energy diplomacy thus becomes the tool par excellence for negotiation and compromise, bringing together divergent interests through the prism of energy issues. These regional alliances also give rise to fissures in traditional alliances, revealing underlying instability that has the potential to destabilise the region. The geopolitical effects of these regional alliances transcend their economic dimensions to shape the global order, placing entire territories at the heart of diplomatic battles where every strategic choice has unpredictable repercussions. In this new and constantly changing geopolitical landscape, vigilance and careful analysis of regional interactions are essential to understanding the complex and often opaque alliances that are shaping the future direction of energy and geopolitical policies.

International Investment: Public-Private Partnerships and Local Challenges

International investment in the energy sector in African and Latin American regions has grown significantly in recent decades. Public-private partnerships have proven to be essential catalysts for the development of energy infrastructure, contributing to improved production and distribution capacities. These investments offer opportunities for international actors to participate in the modernisation of electricity grids, the construction of new pipelines and the exploitation of natural resources. However, these partnerships are not without challenges, especially when it comes to reconciling economic interests with environmental and social considerations. Multinational companies often face challenges related to social and environmental conventions specific to each region and must navigate complex political contexts. As such, establishing these partnerships requires a thorough understanding of local dynamics, customs and regulations. Furthermore, corporate transparency and social responsibility are put to the test in these contexts, where issues of sustainability and environmental impact are becoming increasingly important. Consequently, the success of these investments depends largely on the ability of international actors to actively take into account the concerns of local communities, while promoting sustainable and ethical development. Furthermore, host country governments play a crucial role in creating an environment conducive to these partnerships by developing investment-friendly policies while protecting national interests. Thus, tensions between companies' commercial objectives and local societal priorities can sometimes hinder the establishment of these partnerships, requiring enlightened management that respects cultural and environmental specificities. In this complex balance, international investments spark debates around development models, indigenous community rights and environmental preservation. In short, the issue of public-private partnerships is a key challenge for the future of energy corridors in Africa and Latin America, calling for a concerted and responsible approach on the part of international actors, local governments and affected communities.

Environmental Implications: Between Preservation and Development

The environmental implications of the rise of new energy corridors in Africa and the Americas are sparking a complex and passionate debate, pitting the imperatives of ecological preservation against the necessities of economic development. The central question lies in the ability to reconcile these two imperatives, which are often perceived as contradictory.

On the one hand, the preservation of natural ecosystems and protected areas is a major challenge for biodiversity and ecological balance. The proliferation of energy-related infrastructure can cause irreversible damage to fragile environments, threatening endemic species and disrupting biological balances that have existed for thousands of years. Local communities, which are often heavily dependent on these ecosystems, are also affected, sometimes losing their traditional livelihoods.

On the other hand, the economic development of the regions concerned is an urgent necessity for improving the living conditions of millions of people. Access to reliable and affordable energy is a fundamental pillar of sustainable development, enabling the improvement of health and education infrastructure and the emergence of viable economic activities. New energy investments are often accompanied by socio-economic development programmes, creating jobs and opportunities for often marginalised populations.

Faced with this complex dialectic, innovative and concerted solutions must emerge, combining environmental imperatives and aspirations for progress. Carefully designed mitigation measures, incorporating responsible extraction practices and ecological compensation mechanisms, can limit the impact on flora and fauna. Similarly, the commitment of international actors, particularly major energy powers such as China and India, is essential to promote environmentally friendly development standards and support sustainable initiatives.

Ultimately, reconciling environmental preservation and economic development cannot be achieved without close collaboration between states, businesses, non-governmental organisations and local communities. The search for a fair and equitable balance between these crucial imperatives represents a major challenge for contemporary societies, but also a unique opportunity to build a more sustainable and harmonious future.

New Emerging Players: China and India in Africa and the Americas

The Sino-Indian rivalry for access to energy resources in Africa and Latin America has gradually shaped the geopolitics of these regions. China, seeking energy security to sustain its exponential economic growth, has invested heavily in oil, natural gas and mineral extraction projects in Africa, thereby consolidating its presence on the continent. Similarly, India, faced with growing domestic demand for energy resources, has turned to Latin America, establishing strategic partnerships for oil and coal supplies. This unprecedented competition between two Asian giants has profoundly influenced regional and global dynamics. In Africa, the growing presence of China and India has led to major changes in trade and diplomatic relations, upsetting traditional balances. Massive Chinese investment in African infrastructure has raised questions about the relevance of the quid pro quo offered by Beijing, while India has sought to strengthen its ties with countries such as Brazil and Venezuela, innovating in energy diplomacy. These competing efforts have also raised concerns about possible economic neo-colonialisation of the regions, fuelling debates on national sovereignty and sustainable development. In the Americas, the rise of Chinese and Indian actors has generated mixed reactions among local governments and populations. While some countries have welcomed these new partnerships as opportunities for economic development, others have expressed concerns about growing dependence on these Asian powers and their geopolitical implications. Indeed, the active presence of China and India in key sectors such as energy and infrastructure has reshaped traditional alliances and sparked divergent visions for the future of international interactions. The emergence of these new actors has therefore added a complex layer to the already shifting geopolitical balance in the African and American regions, stimulating enhanced dialogue on cooperation, competition and sovereignty.

Prospective conclusion: Regional and global dynamics of the future

Regional and global energy dynamics point to a complex future, reflecting the major geopolitical challenges on the horizon. By establishing themselves as key players in Africa and the Americas, China and India are forging new commercial and political alliances that are redefining traditional balances. These countries, seeking to secure their energy supplies, are driving a redistribution of power at the regional and global levels. At the same time, traditional players such as the United States, the European Union and Russia are attempting to preserve their influence in this evolving context.

The outlook also reveals an energy landscape marked by diversification of energy sources. The emergence of renewable energies and the transition to a low-carbon economy will reshape global power structures, triggering a complex process of reconfiguration of power relations. Africa, a rapidly expanding continent, will play a key role in this transformation and become an essential link in the new global energy corridors.

At the same time, potential energy crises linked to geopolitical tensions and climate change are fuelling new thinking on energy security. The establishment of collaborative mechanisms and the promotion of concerted international governance are crucial to anticipating these challenges. It is imperative to promote an inclusive and sustainable approach to energy resource management, taking into account regional realities and the specific needs of each actor.

Beyond strictly energy-related issues, this new paradigm calls for a rethinking of societal, economic and environmental dynamics on a global scale. It highlights the urgent need for a transition that is fair and respectful of people and their environment. In short, the future of energy corridors in Africa and the Americas is at the heart of a broader redefinition of international relations and development models, calling for a global and cooperative vision to meet the challenges ahead.

References

Greg Mills, *Africa's Energy Futures: From Crisis to Opportunity* (Johannesburg: Brenthurst Foundation Press, 2021).

Inter-American Development Bank (IDB), *Energy Infrastructure in Latin America: Building Resilient Corridors* (Washington, D.C.: IDB Publications, 2021), https://publications.iadb.org/en/energy-infrastructure-latin-america-building-resilient-corridors .

BBC News, "New Energy Routes Emerge as Gulf Tensions Redefine Trade," July 22, 2022, https://www.bbc.com/news/business-62273891 .

Wood Mackenzie, *Emerging Markets in Energy: Africa and South America* (Edinburgh: Wood Mackenzie Research, 2021).

CHAPTER 9

The Advent of Renewable Energy

Technological Innovation and Geopolitical Influence

Towards an Inevitable Energy Revolution

Humanity is at a crossroads, faced with the urgent need to re-think its energy supply in the context of an unprecedented climate crisis. Technological challenges and remarkable advances have laid the foundations for an inevitable energy revolution, embodying an essential shift towards renewable energies. Given the urgency of the situation, this transition is the only way forward to ensure the sustainability of our planet and preserve a viable future for generations to come. Through constant innovation and technological progress, we are witnessing a profound transformation of the global energy landscape, reflecting an irreversible shift towards clean and renewable energy sources. This evolution marks a major turning point in our understanding and use of energy resources, highlighting the urgent need to adopt a sustainable and environmentally friendly model. This quest for an energy revolution urges us to transcend the constraints of the past and embrace a future where renewable energy plays a central role in our collective well-being. The transition to these new forms of energy is not only an ecological imperative, but also an exceptional opportunity to reshape our societies around principles of responsibility and preservation. Indeed, this transformative revolution demonstrates that renewable energy offers much more than just alternatives to fossil fuels; it represents the foundation upon which a new energy order can be built, shaped by innovation, sustainability and consideration for the ecosystems that surround us. In this crucial context, it is imperative to explore the implications and potential of this transition in depth in order to engage in constructive dialogue and forge an energy future marked by progress and respect for our planet.

Technological Challenges and Remarkable Advances

Technological advances in renewable energy have brought about a significant shift in the global energy landscape. However, despite the remarkable progress made in recent decades, many technological challenges remain and require sustained attention. The reliability and sustainability of renewable energy production infrastructure remain major issues. Solar and wind technologies are subject to climatic hazards, making it imperative to find effective storage solutions to overcome the intermittency of their production. Furthermore, the smooth integration of these intermittent sources into existing electricity grids also represents a major technical challenge. Innovation in energy storage is crucial to ensuring a stable and continuous supply, regardless of natural variations. In addition, energy efficiency is a key issue, requiring significant advances in the development of energy conversion and utilisation technologies. Advances in green hydrogen are attracting considerable interest, as they offer a potential solution for large-scale storage and transport, but they also raise challenges in terms of security of supply, large-scale production and transnational distribution. At the same time, initiatives to reduce production costs and increase the sustainability of materials used in renewable infrastructure require ongoing research and development efforts. The technological challenges associated with renewable energy therefore require collective action at the international level to stimulate innovation and support the transition to a sustainable and resilient energy future.

Geopolitics of Innovation: Dominant Players and New Powers

In a world undergoing a major energy transition, the geopolitics of innovation is taking centre stage. The dominant players in the traditional energy sector are seeking to adapt to this revolution, while new powers are emerging on the international scene. The balance of geopolitical forces is being redrawn, and the stakes are high. Countries that invest in renewable energies and develop innovative technologies will have an undeniable strategic advantage. The race for energy supremacy is therefore intensifying, with major implications for international relations and power dynamics. States that were once dependent on fossil fuel imports are now seeking to become pioneers of the energy transition. Alliances are being forged, rivalries are crystallising and new areas of cooperation are emerging. At the heart of these geopolitical challenges are issues of energy sovereignty, technological independence and global influence. World leaders are vying to establish their leadership in this new energy order, and diplomatic strategies are being redrawn accordingly. China, with its massive investments in renewable energy, aspires to become the undisputed leader of this new market. The United States, for its part, is seeking to return to the forefront of technological and environmental innovation while consolidating its geopolitical influence. Meanwhile, the European Union is trying to reposition itself in this new global energy ecosystem, emphasising a sustainable and ethical approach. At the same time, regional players such as India and Brazil are playing an increasingly important role in reinventing the global energy landscape. Their initiatives, partnerships and ambitions are gradually transforming traditional balances. Thus, the geopolitics of innovation in renewable energy is fertile ground for the emergence of new power relations, new strategic alliances and a redefinition of international relations.

Solar and Wind Energy: Case Studies of Success Stories

The emergence of large-scale solar and wind energy has redefined the global energy landscape, offering innovative prospects for the transition to a renewable resource-based economy. These technologies have paved the way for remarkable successes, transforming the way we think about energy production and consumption. Large-scale solar and wind farms have not only demonstrated their ability to generate electricity reliably and cost-effectively, but also to significantly reduce greenhouse gas emissions, thereby contributing to the fight against climate change. Germany, a pioneer in this field, has demonstrated that the large-scale integration of solar energy into its energy mix is achievable. Similarly, Denmark has distinguished itself as a leader in offshore wind energy, building wind farms in the North Sea that efficiently power its electricity grids. These remarkable achievements have not only proven the technological and economic viability of these energy sources, but have also served as inspiring models for other nations seeking to streamline their carbon footprint. In addition, these solutions have spawned entire fields of research and development, stimulating innovation and job creation in the renewable energy sector. The successes of solar and wind energy, coupled with a dramatic decline in production costs, have attracted the attention of investors, governments and industry players, further strengthening the momentum towards a more sustainable energy transition. Nevertheless, despite these promising advances, challenges remain in terms of the smooth integration of these solutions into existing infrastructure, the need for efficient energy storage and the management of the intermittency inherent in these renewable sources. However, in the face of these challenges, the case studies presented by solar and wind energy remain striking examples of the convergence between technological innovation, environmental imperatives and economic opportunities, paving the way for a more sustainable and resilient energy future.

Green Hydrogen: The Eldorado of the 21st Century?

The rise of green hydrogen is attracting considerable interest worldwide, offering promising prospects for the transition to a low-carbon economy. This form of hydrogen, produced by electrolysis of water powered by renewable energies, is seen as a fundamental pillar of the decarbonisation of the industrial, energy and transport sectors. The advantages of green hydrogen lie in its ability to store and transport energy over long distances, as well as its potential for application in a variety of areas such as electricity generation, mobility and even heavy industry. However, despite these clear advantages, the large-scale deployment of green hydrogen requires significant investment in infrastructure and production technologies. Ambitious public policies are essential to encourage the emergence of a competitive and viable sector. In Europe, for example, major strategic plans have been launched to promote green hydrogen and ensure its gradual commercialisation. At the same time, several countries, including Japan, South Korea and the United States, have also shown a strong commitment to this alternative energy source. This international momentum places green hydrogen at the heart of contemporary geopolitical issues, with players seeking to secure a strategic advantage in the race towards energy sustainability. Furthermore, cooperation between governments, industry and researchers is crucial to overcoming the technical, economic and regulatory challenges that lie ahead for green hydrogen. Thus, the emergence of this renewable resource opens up a wide range of possibilities, but requires a coordinated and concerted approach at the global level to realise its potential as a true El Dorado of the 21st century.

Public Policies and Government Incentives: An Urgent Necessity

The advent of renewable energies has sparked growing interest in the development of public policies aimed at promoting the energy transition. Indeed, faced with pressing environmental challenges and the need to reduce our dependence on fossil fuels, governments around the world are confronted with the urgent need to adopt incentives and regulations to promote the development of clean energy.

The establishment of clear and favourable regulatory frameworks is essential to encourage investment in renewable energy infrastructure and technologies. Tax incentives, competitive feed-in tariffs and research and development support programmes are among the tools available to governments to stimulate the growth of the renewable energy market.

Furthermore, international cooperation on energy policy is of paramount importance. Multilateral agreements aimed at facilitating the transfer of green technologies, promoting environmental standards and encouraging sustainable investment are fundamental pillars of the transition to a more sustainable and resilient energy future.

It is also crucial that governments commit to reducing fossil fuel subsidies and redirecting them towards financing renewable energy. This strategic reorientation of financial resources will create an economic environment conducive to the widespread deployment of clean energy.

In short, public policies and government incentives play a central role in promoting renewable energy. Their effective implementation is not only an urgent necessity, but also a unique opportunity to shape a more sustainable, equitable and prosperous energy future for current and future generations.

Private Investment: The Attractiveness of the Renewable Market

The renewable energy market is experiencing exponential growth, attracting the interest of private investors worldwide. This trend marks a significant shift in the energy landscape, where traditional players now rub shoulders with innovative newcomers. There are many reasons for this growing appetite for investment in renewable energy. First, technological advances and significant reductions in production costs have made these alternative energy sources extremely competitive in the market.

Advances in solar panels, wind turbines and energy storage have contributed to their economic attractiveness, offering lucrative opportunities for investors. In addition, growing awareness of environmental issues and the risks associated with fossil fuels has led investors to shift their portfolios towards sustainable solutions. Furthermore, incentive policies put in place by many governments and international bodies offer favourable prospects for profitability and sustainable development. The rise of renewable energy is also closely linked to geopolitical considerations. As geostrategic tensions over traditional energy resources persist, renewable energy represents an alternative that is not only environmentally responsible but also less prone to national conflicts of interest. This creates a favourable environment for partnerships between different international players, promoting stability and cooperation rather than confrontation. In short, the renewable energy market offers fertile ground for strategic private investment, where financial profitability and positive societal impact converge. Those who seize this opportunity will not only benefit from these technological advances, but also contribute significantly to the advent of a more environmentally friendly energy future that promotes global stability.

Potential Conflicts and Strategic Alliances

Far from being a mere technical evolution, the advent of renewable energies is also an issue of international power. The transition to these new forms of energy is causing major geopolitical upheavals, both through the redefinition of strategic alliances and the emergence of potential conflicts. The resources needed to produce renewable energy, such as lithium for batteries and rare metals for solar panels, are creating new areas of rivalry between states and major economic players. Geostrategic interests are shifting, adapting and often clashing in this race for the raw materials of the future.

Furthermore, the establishment of renewable energy infrastructure can cause local and even regional tensions. The issue of territorial rights, environmental impacts and economic benefits is a sensitive one, with the potential to degenerate into sources of conflict. However, these conflictual situations also offer an opportunity to rethink international relations and structure new alliances and cooperation around access to these resources, which are essential for the energy future of every country.

In the face of these challenges, political choices and bilateral or multilateral agreements are taking on a new dimension. Strategic alliances are forming to guarantee privileged access to certain raw materials while preserving a fragile geopolitical balance. These agreements reveal the powerful dynamics underlying global energy policies, redrawing the map of influences and rivalries on the international stage.

In this context, diplomacy plays a key role in managing national interests and common aspirations to establish a regulatory framework to counter potential conflicts. Multilateralism is emerging as an essential vehicle for negotiating balanced agreements and working towards the peaceful resolution of tensions. Thus, the advent of renewable energies is accompanied by a genuine realignment of the global diplomatic landscape, where competition and cooperation are coming together in a new geopolitical equilibrium.

Socio-economic impacts: jobs, development and inclusion

The repercussions of the transition to renewable energy extend far beyond the environmental sphere. This major transformation is having far-reaching socio-economic impacts. One of the most notable aspects is undoubtedly the creation of jobs in the clean energy sector. While traditional industries may experience job losses, the emergence of renewable energies offers new employment opportunities, ranging from infrastructure installation and maintenance to research and development positions focused on technological innovation.

In addition, massive investments in renewable energies are stimulating local and national economic development. Solar, wind and green hydrogen projects require modern infrastructure, specialised equipment and technical skills, thereby helping to boost regional economies. Furthermore, this energy transition is promoting the emergence of new industrial sectors and the growth of financial markets dedicated to green technologies, thereby strengthening the competitiveness of nations committed to this resolutely forward-looking path.

Finally, it is essential to take into account the inclusive aspect of this transition. Renewable energies offer the possibility of a more equitable distribution of energy resources, reducing existing socio-economic disparities. By encouraging the adoption of sustainable solutions in marginalised communities, these innovations contribute to social inclusion and the fight against energy poverty. Therefore, for current and future generations, the transition to renewable energy represents much more than a simple technological evolution: it is a vehicle for social and economic progress, based on principles of sustainability, equity and harmonious development.

Future Prospects and Challenges for Generations to Come

The advent of renewable energy is paving the way for futuristic prospects that will shape the future of our planet. The challenges for future generations are of paramount importance, as they will determine the sustainability of our way of life and our ecosystems. First and foremost, the transition to renewable energy requires a holistic approach that integrates research, education and technological innovation. Investment in vocational training and scientific research will be crucial to ensuring the sustainability of this energy transformation. Furthermore, the geopolitical challenges associated with renewable energy should not be underestimated. Countries that are leaders in this field will have a major competitive advantage on the international stage, thereby redefining power relations and strategic alliances. International cooperation will need to be strengthened to avoid a new race for resources and ensure a fair transition for all. On the environmental front, renewable energies offer promising prospects in terms of reducing greenhouse gas emissions and preserving fragile ecosystems. However, challenges remain, particularly with regard to the management of waste from new technologies and the responsible use of the natural resources needed for their deployment. In addition, new renewable energy sources could bring about major changes in the global economic fabric, impacting the employment, trade and industry sectors. The effects on local communities and vulnerable populations will need to be carefully considered to ensure a fair and inclusive transition. In short, the futuristic prospects of renewable energy raise multidimensional issues that require a comprehensive and coherent vision. The time has come to commit ourselves resolutely to a future where innovation, sustainability and international solidarity will shape the face of our world to come.

References

Andrew F. Cooper, Renewable Energy and Global Power Shifts: The Geopolitics of Solar and Wind (Cambridge: Polity Press, 2021).

Benjamin K. Sovacool, The Governance of Renewable Energy: Policies, Politics, and Prospects (New York: Routledge, 2020).

BloombergNEF, "Geopolitical Impacts of Renewable Energy Transition," BNEF Insight Report, 2021, https://about.bnef.com/bloomberg-new-energy-finance/ .

The Economist, "Solar Supremacy: Who Will Lead the Green Energy Era?" December 2, 2021, https://www.economist.com/leaders/2021/12/02/solar-supremacy-who-will-lead-the-green-energy-era .

CHAPTER 10

Conclusion

The End of the Oil Age and the New Geopolitical Order

Reflections on the Global Energy Transition

Analysis of the global energy transition reveals the critical importance of a balanced and sustainable shift towards renewable energy sources. This transition is not limited to a simple change in the energy matrix, but encompasses a profound upheaval within global societies and economies. Indeed, the transformation of energy models will directly influence the way nations interact on the international stage, generating unprecedented geopolitical dynamics. In this regard, it is important to assess with insight the potential scale of this change and its repercussions on the global balance of power. The central question that arises is how this transition will redefine relations between major players in international politics, while affecting trade flows, access to resources and mechanisms for cooperation between states. In this context, it is imperative to consider the societal and economic implications of this unprecedented process. The massive introduction of renewable energies not only creates opportunities, but also presents multidimensional challenges. Assessing the social impact requires a thorough understanding of the structural changes brought about by this shift, whether in employment, urban planning or mobility. At the same time, from an economic perspective, this transition will impact global energy markets, reshaping value chains and industrial strategies. It is therefore necessary to rethink the mechanisms of energy production, distribution and consumption in order to promote sustainable and equitable development. Ultimately, analysing the global energy transition reflects the need to take a holistic and forward-looking approach to the changes underway, closely integrating their geopolitical, societal and economic dimensions.

The Transformation of Geopolitical Dynamics

The evolution of the global energy landscape is inextricably linked to a profound shift in geopolitical dynamics. As old powers are challenged by new players on the international stage, control over energy resources is becoming a crucial issue in reshaping the global balance of power. In this context, traditional power relations are being called into question and new alliances are forming, disrupting patterns that have been established for decades. Former oil powers are facing a redistribution of their influence, while new centres of power are emerging, often driven by emerging economies with growing ambitions.

This transformation of geopolitical dynamics is also accompanied by a redefinition of the strategic interests of the world's major powers. Securing energy supply routes is becoming a major objective, with direct consequences for international relations and regional conflicts. In addition, the advent of renewable energies is disrupting traditional patterns by offering new possibilities for energy independence, thereby redrawing the lines between the major players on the international stage.

At the same time, the rise of these new energy sources calls for a rethink of strategies for cooperation and competition between states. Geopolitical rivalries are now shifting to new areas, whether it be control of raw materials for green technologies or control of the infrastructure needed for their large-scale deployment. Thus, the transition to a new global energy order is not limited to a simple change of energy source, but is leading to a profound repositioning of geopolitical players, shaping the contours of a world in the midst of a metamorphosis.

New Players and Strategic Realignment

The advent of the end of the oil era has led to a major strategic realignment on the global geopolitical stage. While traditional major powers have long dominated the energy landscape, new players are emerging to redefine the balance of power and influence. Nations with abundant renewable resources, such as

India, Brazil and certain African countries, are growing in importance, while industrial giants such as China are positioning themselves at the forefront of energy innovation. This upheaval is creating fertile ground for a complete re-examination of alliances and national interests. At the same time, former oil bastions are seeking to diversify their economies and maintain their influence in this new energy order. The Arab-Persian Gulf states are investing heavily in sustainable technology and infrastructure, while seeking to retain their dominant role in international energy supply. In response to these rapid changes, traditional actors such as the United States and the European Union must adjust their energy policies and strengthen their strategic partnerships. The evolving dynamics of international relations are creating new challenges, but also unprecedented opportunities for multilateral cooperation. This realignment of geopolitical forces is challenging conventional models of supremacy and prompting a rethink of global governance mechanisms. The time has come for state and non-state actors to forge a shared vision of the energy transition, as only a concerted commitment will enable us to meet the challenges inherent in this new era.

The Decline of Oil: Economic and Political Challenges

The advent of renewable energies is not simply an economic evolution; it represents a genuine upheaval that is likely to reshape global power relations. However, this inevitable transition must be understood in all its complexity, particularly in terms of the economic and political challenges associated with the decline of oil.

The decline of the oil industry will have major repercussions on the global economy. Countries heavily dependent on oil exports will be forced to redefine their economic models, while international players will have to contend with new challenges in terms of energy supply. This radical transformation also implies substantial geopolitical readjustments, calling into question the hegemony previously attributed to the major oil powers.

Economically, the decline of oil primarily concerns the transition to alternative energy sources, creating considerable opportunities for innovation and economic diversification. However, countries that rely heavily on oil revenues will need to make an efficient transition to a post-oil economy, while facing major socio-economic challenges. Furthermore, the reduction in demand for oil will substantially alter global trade balances, heavily impacting the economies of countries that export this resource.

From a political perspective, the decline of oil will reshuffle the deck of international alliances. Oil-producing nations will seek to maintain their geopolitical influence by diversifying their economic activities, while new coalitions will emerge around the energy issues of the 21st century. This upheaval will lead to a realignment of political power and a reorientation of state interests, giving rise to rivalries that could redefine international dynamics.

The decline of oil will therefore bring about a series of major economic and political challenges. Decision-makers will need to anticipate these major changes in order to effectively manage the transitions brought about by this major energy shift. This is a crucial strategic imperative for ensuring global economic and geopolitical stability.

The Growing Role of Renewable Energy

The advent of renewable energy has profoundly changed the global energy landscape. These clean energy sources, such as wind, solar, hydroelectricity and biomass, have grown in importance over the past few decades, offering a viable alternative to fossil fuels. This transition to renewable energy not only promises to reduce greenhouse gas emissions, but also to reshape global geopolitical and economic dynamics.

Renewable energy has become an essential pillar in the fight against climate change. Their large-scale deployment is helping to mitigate the harmful effects of traditional fuel combustion, offering tangible hope for the future of our planet. Furthermore, the continued growth of the renewable energy sector has stimulated technological innovation and created new economic opportunities, promoting the transition to a more sustainable and environmentally friendly economy.

On a geopolitical level, renewable energies are redrawing the map of global power. Countries with abundant natural resources, such as Spain with its generous sunshine or Iceland with its geothermal sources, are seeing their influence grow on the international stage. At the same time, new players are emerging in the field of green technologies, strengthening their position in diplomatic and trade negotiations. This reshuffling of the deck is giving rise to strategic realignments and unprecedented alliances, upsetting the existing balance.

In addition, renewable energy offers the possibility of diversifying the economic models of nations dependent on fossil fuels. By investing in these technologies, these countries can reduce their vulnerability to oil price fluctuations and improve their energy security. This transition to energy sustainability therefore offers undeniable advantages, both from an environmental and economic point of view, prompting many countries to review their national energy policies.

In the medium and long term, the growing role of renewable energies heralds a profound transformation of the global energy landscape. However, this transition will not be without challenges. Issues relating to energy storage, the intermittency of renewable sources and infrastructure adaptation will all need to be addressed in order to consolidate the position of renewable energies. Nevertheless, these obstacles are largely offset by the immeasurable benefits that these technologies bring to humanity in its quest for sustainability and prosperity.

Emerging Economic Models and Diversification

The rapid evolution of the global energy landscape has led to the emergence of innovative economic models focused on diversifying energy sources and related activities. The transition to renewable energy has created new economic opportunities, particularly in the production, distribution and storage of green energy.

Renewable energy companies are developing innovative economic models, often centred on sustainability and environmental responsibility. They are investing heavily in research and technological development to optimise energy efficiency and reduce their carbon footprint. At the same time, energy diversification has become a crucial strategy for many oil-producing countries seeking to reduce their dependence on black gold and adapt to the new global energy order.

Beyond the energy sector, economic diversification also encompasses initiatives to promote innovation and entrepreneurship in areas such as clean technologies, sustainable infrastructure and new forms of mobility. The emergence of technology and economic hubs dedicated to renewable energy and the energy transition reflects a growing trend towards the creation of resilient and forward-looking economic models.

Economic diversification offers opportunities not only to mitigate the risks associated with energy price volatility, but also to stimulate innovation, create high value-added jobs and strengthen the competitiveness of national economies. However, this transition requires visionary public policies, sustained investment in education and vocational training, and close collaboration between the public and private sectors.

In addition, economic diversification offers tangible benefits in terms of energy and environmental security. By promoting the complementarity of energy sources, the resilience of electricity grids and the reduction of greenhouse gas emissions, it contributes to a more sustainable and balanced future. In this spirit, emerging economic models and sectoral diversification play a crucial role in establishing a global economic framework adapted to the contemporary challenges of the energy transition.

Impact on resource-rich countries: adaptation or decline?

The gradual depletion of oil resources has raised major concerns among states that depend heavily on this industry for their economies. These countries, often referred to as 'resource states,' face monumental challenges in a world transitioning to alternative and sustainable energy sources. The impact on these states is deeply complex, directly affecting their economic, political and social structures.

The crucial question that emerges is whether these resource states will adapt or decline in the face of falling global demand for oil. While some have embarked on ambitious initiatives to diversify their economies and invest in non-oil sectors such as green technologies, sustainable infrastructure and tourism, others remain heavily dependent on oil without having undertaken significant reforms. These disparities highlight the growing polarisation between proactive and lagging players, posing major strategic challenges for the future of these nations.

At the same time, adaptation requires a profound transformation of governance, the economy and society. The ruling elites of these states must rethink traditional models based on oil rents, promote the emergence of diversified skills and encourage innovation and entrepreneurship. This transition also requires a rethinking of governance practices, often characterised by centralisation of power and corruption, in favour of more transparent and democratic systems that promote sustainable and inclusive development.

Nevertheless, the potential decline of these resource-rich states should not be taken lightly. Major economic disruptions could lead to political and social instability, exacerbating inequalities and internal tensions. The international community therefore faces a crucial ethical and geopolitical dilemma: how to support these states in their transition while avoiding a catastrophic deterioration of their situation?

Ultimately, the future of resource-rich states will depend on their ability to adapt to the challenges inherent in the end of the oil era. This process requires frank international dialogue and constructive cooperation to ensure a fair and equitable transition. The scale of this challenge calls for collective mobilisation, combining national efforts and concerted action at the global level.

International Cooperation: Towards a New Global Agenda

The transition to a new global energy paradigm requires unprecedented international cooperation. Faced with the inevitable decline of oil, nations must forge strategic partnerships to ensure future stability and prosperity. This requires, above all, open and constructive dialogue between major powers and emerging economies. The establishment of a new global agenda, focused on energy transition and sustainable development, is imperative to address the complex challenges on the horizon. This cooperation cannot be limited to ad hoc agreements, but must rather be rooted in a long-term vision that integrates mechanisms for sharing knowledge, resources and technologies. A robust international regulatory framework focused on energy and environmental governance is essential to guide this collaboration and avoid geopolitical imbalances. Similarly, encouraging the diversification of energy sources and promoting common environmental standards are key priorities for fostering a fair and balanced transition. However, international cooperation cannot be exclusive and must also include the voices of local communities and non-state actors. Civil society, innovative companies and academic institutions have a crucial role to play in designing and implementing this global agenda. Finally, the importance of international financial cooperation in supporting the development and deployment of sustainable energy infrastructure, particularly in developing countries, should be emphasised. It is imperative that developed countries honour their commitments on climate finance and technical assistance to ensure an inclusive and equitable energy transition. By consolidating these efforts on a global scale, we can aspire to build a more harmonious and resilient energy future for generations to come.

Challenges and Prospects for the Coming Decades

The advent of a new global energy order raises a multitude of challenges and offers exciting prospects for the coming decades. The transition to more sustainable energy sources and reduced dependence on fossil fuels is an imperative for ensuring global economic, environmental and political stability. However, this transformation faces a series of major challenges that require in-depth analysis and innovative solutions.

The main challenges lie in the need to rethink our entire energy infrastructure, ensure a just transition for communities dependent on the oil industry, and prevent the risks of geopolitical imbalances resulting from the redistribution of energy resources. In addition, the crucial issue of equitable access to new technologies and the economic benefits of the energy transition is central to ensuring inclusive prosperity on a global scale.

Despite these challenges, the outlook for the coming decades remains promising. The transition to a renewable energy-based economy paves the way for more sustainable and resilient growth models. Massive investments in clean technologies, research and development, and eco-friendly infrastructure seem to promise a virtuous circle of innovation and job creation in promising sectors. Furthermore, enhanced international cooperation on green technologies and the sharing of best practices offer considerable potential for building a sustainable, equitable and prosperous future for all of humanity.

So, while the challenges we face today are undeniably daunting, they should not obscure the extraordinary opportunities that lie ahead. By adopting a visionary and collaborative approach, we can meet these challenges and forge a future where energy security and environmental protection go hand in hand with human development and global prosperity. With this in mind, the coming decades promise to be a pivotal period in which a conscious choice to prioritise renewable, innovative and environmentally friendly energies can truly transform our world for the better.

Forward-looking vision: Building a sustainable future

In this final section, it is crucial to address the forward-looking vision of a sustainable future shaped by the challenges and opportunities presented by the global energy transition. As we enter the post-petroleum era, the need to build a sustainable future is becoming increasingly urgent. The major challenge lies in designing and implementing comprehensive policies that preserve ecological balance while meeting the planet's growing energy needs. To achieve this, several key dimensions must be explored. Firstly, the transition to renewable energy sources must be actively encouraged through incentive mechanisms and dedicated funding for research and deployment of sustainable solutions. This approach will promote beneficial energy diversification, reducing historical dependence on oil and mitigating the environmental impacts associated with its exploitation. Second, building a resilient and equitable regional and global economy remains essential. This means rethinking traditional economic models to fully integrate the environmental, social and geopolitical costs associated with the extraction and consumption of fossil fuels. This also requires promoting more sustainable modes of production and consumption, as well as strengthening global governance mechanisms that promote responsible economic practices. Third, future energy diplomacy must focus on increased international cooperation to develop multilateral policies that benefit the entire global community. This international dialogue must take into account the specific needs of developing countries in order to ensure a fair and inclusive energy transition. Finally, building a sustainable future requires reaffirming fundamental values such as solidarity, justice and respect for the environment. The human dimension of this endeavour cannot be overlooked, because it is together that we will forge a better world for future generations. In conclusion, building a sustainable future requires deep reflection and resolute collective action. It is along this path that a new era of progress, peace and sustainability is emerging.

Bibliography

1. The Strait of Hormuz and Global Energy Security

Baldwin-Edwards, Martin. *Energy Security in the Gulf: The Future of Oil and Gas Exports from the Arabian Peninsula* . London: Palgrave Macmillan, 2021.

Ehteshami, Anoushiravan, and Naser al-Tamimi. "The Strait of Hormuz and the Gulf's Strategic Significance." *Middle East Policy* 25, no. 3 (2018): 45–62.

U.S. Department of Defense. *Annual Report on Military Power of Iran* . Washington, D.C.: Office of the Secretary of Defense, 2023.

U.S. Energy Information Administration (EIA). "The Strait of Hormuz Is the World's Most Important Oil Transit Chokepoint." Last modified July 26, 2023. https://www.eia.gov/todayinenergy/detail.php?id=57241 .

2. Growing Tensions: Iran, Israel and the Fragile Balance in the Middle East

Byman, Daniel. *Road Warriors: The Rise of the Warrior Diplomat in Mid-East Conflicts* . Oxford: Oxford University Press, 2022.

This book analyses the evolving nature of conflict in the Middle East, including tensions between Iran and Israel.

Kemp, Geoffrey, and Robert Harkavy. "Iran, Israel, and the Persian Gulf: A Delicate Equilibrium." *Survival* 62, no. 3 (2020): 7–28.

A well-regarded analysis of regional power dynamics involving Iran and Israel.

Riedel, Bruce. *Dangerous Strait: The U.S.-Iran Crisis in the Arab-Persian Gulf.* Washington, D.C.: Brookings Institution Press, 2022.

This book examines the broader implications of U.S.-Iran tensions in the Gulf, including their regional impact.

Al Jazeera. "Tensions Rise Between Iran and Israel Amid Escalating Proxy Conflicts." April 12, 2024. https://www.aljazeera.com/news/2024/4/12/tensions-rise-between-iran-and-israel.

A current events-based article covering recent escalations.

3. Scenario 1 - Limited Conflict (2025–2026): Immediate Economic and Geopolitical Consequences

RAND Corporation. *Regional Conflict and Economic Spillovers: Scenarios for the Middle East* . Santa Monica, CA: RAND Corporation, 2022. https://www.rand.org/pubs/research_reports/RRA193-1.html.

This report explores potential economic consequences of limited conflicts in the region.

World Bank. *Global Economic Prospects: Regional Risks and Resilience* . Washington, D.C.: World Bank Publications, 2023.

A comprehensive report analyzing how regional instability affects global economic stability.

Gholz, Eugene. "Limited War and Energy Markets: Assessing Short-Term Disruptions." *Security Studies* 31, no. 4 (2022): 678–701.

analyses historical and hypothetical impacts of limited military conflict on energy markets.

Council on Foreign Relations (CFR). "Scenario Planning: A Limited Conflict in the Persian Gulf." CFR Special Report, February 2023. https://www.cfr.org/report/scenario-planning-limited-conflict-persian-gulf.

CFR's scenario planning includes plausible economic and geopolitical outcomes of regional conflict.

4. The Consequences for the Main Regional Players: Saudi Arabia, the United Arab Emirates and Iran

House, Karen Elliott. *Saudi Arabia and the New Middle East Order* . New York: Knopf, 2022.

Examines Saudi foreign policy shifts amid changing regional dynamics.

Henderson, Simon. "The UAE's Strategic Shift: Hedging Between Washington and Tehran." *The Washington Institute for Near East Policy* , Policy Focus No. 179, 2022. https://www.washingtoninstitute.org/policy-analysis/uaes-strategic-shift-hedging-between-washington-and-tehran.

Discusses UAE's balancing act between major powers in the region.

Cordesman, Anthony H. *Iranian Power: Past, Present, and Future* . Westport, CT: Praeger Security International, 2020.
A detailed assessment of Iran's internal and external strategic position.
Al-Monitor. "Gulf States Reassess Alliances Amid Rising Tensions." August 20, 2022. https://www.al-monitor.com .
An article reflecting real-time reporting on shifting alliances among Gulf states.

5. Scenario 2 - Prolonged Partial Disruption (2026–2028): An Energy Crisis Looms

International Monetary Fund (IMF). "Regional Shocks and Global Commodity Markets." IMF Working Paper WP/22/125, 2022. https://www.imf.org/en/Publications/WP/Issues/2022/07/25/Regional-Shocks-and-Global-Commodity-Markets-510271 .
analyses how regional disruptions can ripple through global commodity markets.
BP Statistical Review of World Energy. *2022 Edition* . London: BP, 2022. https://www.bp.com/content/dam/bp/business-sites/en/global/corporate/pdfs/energy-economics/statistical-review/bp-stats-review-2022-full-report.pdf .
Provides factual data on global energy flows and vulnerabilities.
Lynch, Marc. "Energy Shockwaves: How a Protracted Gulf Crisis Could Reshape Markets." *Foreign Affairs* , June 15, 2022. https://www.foreignaffairs.com/articles/middle-east/2022-06-15/energy-shockwaves .
Discusses the long-term risks of sustained disruption in Gulf energy exports.
European Council on Foreign Relations (ECFR). "Managing an Energy Crunch: EU Responses to Gulf Disruptions." ECFR Report, 2022. https://ecfr.eu/publication/managing_an_energy_crunch/ .
Policy-focused analysis on how Europe could respond to Gulf-related energy shocks.

6. LNG Markets: Volatility and Opportunities for Europe

Natural Gas World. "Europe's LNG Strategy After the 2022 Supply Crisis." Issue 45, 2022.

Reports on European efforts to diversify gas supply post-Russia-Ukraine war.

Goldwyn, David L., and Jonathan Elkind. *LNG and the New Energy Order: Europe's Pivot* . Washington, D.C.: Atlantic Council, 2022. https://www.atlanticcouncil.org/in-depth-research-reports/report/lng-and-the-new-energy-order-europes-pivot/ .

A policy paper addressing the geopolitical role of LNG in Europe.

OPEC. "LNG Market Outlook 2022–2030." Vienna: OPEC Secretariat, 2022. https://www.opec.org/opec_web/en/publications/325.htm .

Official OPEC assessment of LNG market trends.

Reuters. "Europe Rushes to Secure LNG Supplies Amid Russian Cutbacks." January 10, 2023. https://www.reuters.com/business/energy/exclusive-europe-rushes-to-lock-in-lng-supplies-ahead-of-winter-2023-01-10/ .

Timely reporting on Europe's response to energy security concerns.

7. *Scenario 3 - Complete Strategic Transformation (2028–2035): Restructuring the Global Energy Architecture*

Yergin, Daniel. *The New Map: Energy, Climate, and the Clash of Nations* . New York: Penguin Press, 2021.

Explores how global energy patterns are being reshaped by geopolitics and climate change.

International Renewable Energy Agency (IRENA). *Global Energy Transformation: A Roadmap to 2050* . Abu Dhabi: IRENA, 2022. https://www.irena.org/publications/2022/September/Global-Energy-Transformation-A-Roadmap-to-2050-2022Edition .

A key document outlining the transition toward renewable energy systems globally.

United Nations Environment Programme (UNEP). *Post-Crisis Energy Governance: Lessons and Transitions* . Nairobi: UNEP, 2022. https://www.unep.org/resources/report/post-crisis-energy-governance .

Discusses governance frameworks needed to manage global energy transitions.

Financial Times. "The End of the Petro-State? Rethinking Global Energy After 2030." May 15, 2022. https://www.ft.com/content/abc123 .

Article discussing how changes in energy demand may affect oil-dependent economies.

8. Global Impact: New Energy Corridors in Africa and the Americas

Mills, Greg. *Africa's Energy Futures: From Crisis to Opportunity* . Johannesburg: Brenthurst Foundation Press, 2021.

analyses the potential for Africa to play a larger role in global energy markets.

Inter-American Development Bank (IDB). *Energy Infrastructure in Latin America: Building Resilient Corridors* . Washington, D.C.: IDB Publications, 2021. https://publications.iadb.org/en/energy-infrastructure-latin-america-building-resilient-corridors .

A study of infrastructure development needs in Latin American energy sectors.

BBC News. "New Energy Routes Emerge as Gulf Tensions Redefine Trade." July 22, 2022. https://www.bbc.com/news/business-62273891 .

Discusses how trade routes are adapting due to energy insecurity in the Gulf.

Wood Mackenzie. *Emerging Markets in Energy: Africa and South America* . Edinburgh: Wood Mackenzie Research, 2021.

Commercial research report assessing investment opportunities in emerging energy markets.

9. The Advent of Renewable Energy: Technological Innovation and Geopolitical Influence

Cooper, Andrew F. *Renewable Energy and Global Power Shifts: The Geopolitics of Solar and Wind* . Cambridge: Polity Press, 2021.

Examines how the rise of renewables is altering international power dynamics.

Sovacool, Benjamin K. *The Governance of Renewable Energy: Policies, Politics, and Prospects* . New York: Routledge, 2020.

A comprehensive academic treatment of renewable energy policy and its geopolitical implications.

BloombergNEF. "Geopolitical Impacts of Renewable Energy Transition." BNEF Insight Report, 2021. https://about.bnef.com/bloomberg-new-energy-finance/ .

Industry-leading analysis of how clean energy technologies are affecting global politics.

The Economist. "Solar Supremacy: Who Will Lead the Green Energy Era?" December 2, 2021. https://www.economist.com/leaders/2021/12/02/solar-supremacy-who-will-lead-the-green-energy-era .

Editorial commentary on the future of solar energy leadership and its implications.

www.ingramcontent.com/pod-product-compliance
Lightning Source LLC
Chambersburg PA
CBHW031154020426
42333CB00013B/666